MCA

Microsoft® Office Specialist (Office 365 and Office 2019)

Study Guide

Excel Associate Exam MO-200

Eric Butow

SYBEX®
A Wiley Brand

To my family and friends

Acknowledgments

I have many people to thank, starting with my literary agent, Matt Wagner. He connected me with Sybex to write this book and managed our relationship well. Next, I want to give a shout-out to my excellent editing team: Gary Schwartz, Barath Kumar Rajasekaran, Christine O'Connor, and Senior Acquisitions Editor Kenyon Brown.

And, as always, I want to thank my family and friends for their everlasting support. I couldn't write this book without them.

—Eric Butow

About the Author

 **Eric Butow** is the owner of Butow Communications Group (BCG) in Jackson, California. BCG offers website development, online marketing, and technical writing services. Eric is a native Californian who started working with his friend's Apple II Plus and Radio Shack TRS-80 Model III in 1980 when he lived in Fresno, California. He learned about programming, graphic design, and desktop publishing in the Fresno PC Users Group in his professional career and when he started BCG in 1994.

Eric has written 37 other technical books as an author, as a co-author or, in one case, as a ghostwriter. Most of Eric's works were written for the general book market, but some were written for specific clients, including HP and F5 Networks. Two of his books have been translated into Chinese and Italian. Eric's most recent books are *Programming Interviews for Dummies* (For Dummies, 2019) with John Sonmez, *Instagram for Dummies* (For Dummies, 2019) with Jennifer Herman and Corey Walker, and *Ultimate Guide to Social Media Marketing* (Entrepreneur Press, 2020) with Jenn Herman, Stephanie Liu, Amanda Robinson, and Mike Allton.

Upon his graduation from California State University, Fresno in 1996 with a master's degree in communication, Eric moved to Roseville, California, where he lived for 13 years. Eric continued to build his business and worked as a technical writer for a wide variety of businesses, from startups to large companies, including Intel, Wells Fargo Wachovia, TASQ Technology, Cisco Systems, and Hewlett-Packard. Many of those clients required their technical writers to know Microsoft Excel, which Eric has used since the early 1990s. From 1997 to 1999, during his off-time, Eric produced 30 issues of *Sacra Blue*, the award-winning monthly magazine of the Sacramento PC Users Group.

When Eric isn't working in (and on) his business or writing books, you can find him enjoying time with friends, walking around the historic Gold Rush town of Jackson, and helping his mother manage her infant and toddler daycare business.

About the Technical Editor

Kristen Merritt is an experienced technical editor who has reviewed books for several publishers, including Wiley and Microsoft Press. Kristen spent 12 years in technical sales, and she is currently employed as a digital marketer.

Contents at a Glance

Contents

Table of Exercises

Introduction

Welcome to *MCA Microsoft Office Specialist (Office 365 and Office 2019) Study Guide: Excel Associate Exam MO-200!* This book is the first step in your journey to becoming a Microsoft Certified Office Specialist for Microsoft Excel, which is a component of the Microsoft 365 suite of productivity applications to which you can subscribe. You can also use this book with the one-time purchase version of Excel, which Microsoft calls Excel 2019.

Microsoft 365 allows you to use the different versions of Excel on many platforms, including Windows, macOS, iOS, iPadOS, and Android. You can even use the web version of Excel on the free online version of Microsoft 365. This book, however, talks about using the most popular version of Excel on the most popular operating system, which happens to be Excel for Microsoft 365 running on Windows 10.

You may already know about a lot of Excel features by working with it, but regardless of whether you use Excel for your regular documentation tasks or you're new to the application, you'll learn a lot about the power that Excel gives you to create all kinds of documents.

Who Should Read This Book

If you want to prepare to take the Microsoft Excel Exam MO-200, which will help you become a certified Excel specialist and hopefully increase your stature, marketability, and income, then this is the book for you. Even if you're not going to take the exam but you want to learn how to use Excel more effectively, this book will show you how to get the most out of using Excel based on features that Microsoft believes are important for you to know.

What You'll Learn from This Book

What you learn in this book adheres to the topics in the Microsoft Excel Exam MO-200, because this book is designed to help you learn about the topics in the exam and pass it on the first try.

After you finish reading the book and complete all the exercises, you'll have an in-depth understanding of Excel that you can use to become more productive at work and at home (or in your home office).

Hardware and Software Requirements

You should be running a computer with Windows 10 installed, and you should have Excel for Microsoft 365 or Excel 2019 installed and running too before you dive into this book. Either version of Excel contains all the features that are documented in this book so that you can pass the exam.

How to Use This Book

Start by taking the Assessment Test after this introduction to see how well you know Excel already. Even if you've been using Excel for a while, you may be surprised at how much you don't know about it.

Next, read each chapter and go through each of the exercises in the chapter to reinforce the concepts in each section. When you reach the end of the chapter, answer each of the 10 Review Questions to test what you learned. You can check your answers in the appendix at the back of the book.

If you're indeed taking the exam, then there are two other valuable tools that you can use: Flashcards and a Practice Exam. You may remember flashcards from when you were in school, and they're useful when you want to reinforce your knowledge. Use the Flashcards with a friend or relative if you like. (They might appreciate learning about Excel, too.) The Practice Exam will help you further hone your ability to answer any question on the real exam with no worries.

How to Contact Wiley or the Author

If you believe you have found an error in this book and it is not listed on the book's errata page, you can report the issue to our customer technical support team at support. wiley.com.

You can email the author with your comments or questions at eric@butow.net. You can also visit Eric's website at www.butow.net.

How This Book Is Organized

Chapter 1: Managing Worksheets and Workbooks   This chapter introduces you to importing data into workbooks, navigating within a workbook, formatting worksheets and workbooks so that they look the way you want, customizing Excel options and views, saving a workbook, sharing a workbook, and inspecting a workbook before you share it, so that all of your recipients can read it.

Chapter 2: Using Data Cells and Ranges   This chapter follows up by showing you how to manipulate your data in a worksheet to show the data that you want to see; formatting cells and ranges in a worksheet using Excel tools, including Format Painter and styles; defining and referencing cell ranges; and summarizing your data with Sparklines and conditional formatting.

Chapter 3: Working with Tables and Table Data   This chapter shows you how to use the built-in table tools to create tables of information, convert the table to a cell range (and vice versa), as well as modify the table to look the way that you want. You'll also learn how to sort and filter text in a table.

Chapter 4: Performing Operations by Using Formulas and Functions   This chapter tells you how to insert references into a cell formula, perform calculations, count cells, execute conditional operations, as well as format text using a variety of built-in Excel functions.

Chapter 5: Managing Charts   This chapter covers how to create charts within a worksheet and on a separate worksheet, modify a chart to show the data you want, format a chart with layouts and styles, and add alternative text to a chart so that everyone who sees the chart will know what it's about.

Interactive Online Learning Environment and Test Bank

Learning the material in the *MCA Microsoft Office Specialist (Office 365 and Office 2019) Study Guide: Excel Associate Exam MO-200* is an important part of preparing for the *Excel Exam MO-200*, but we also provide additional tools to help you prepare. The online test bank will help you understand the types of questions that will appear on the certification exam.

The sample tests in the test bank include all of the questions in each chapter as well as the questions from the Assessment Test. In addition, there is a Practice Exam containing 50 questions. You can use this test to evaluate your understanding and identify areas that may require additional study.

The flashcards in the test bank will push the limits of what you should know for the certification exam. The flashcards contain 100 questions provided in digital format. Each flashcard has one question and one correct answer.

The online glossary is a searchable list of key terms introduced in this Study Guide that you should know for the *Excel Exam MO-200*.

To start using these tools to study for the *MCA Microsoft Office Specialist Study Guide: Excel Exam MO-200*, go to www.wiley.com/go/sybextestprep and register your book to receive your unique PIN. Once you have the PIN, return to www.wiley.com/go/sybextestprep, find your book, and click Register, or log in and follow the link to register a new account or to add this book to an existing account.

Exam objectives are subject to change at any time without prior notice and at Microsoft's sole discretion. Please visit the Exam MO-200: Microsoft Excel (Excel and Excel 2019) website (https://docs.microsoft.com/en-us/learn/certifications/exams/MO-200) for the most current listing of exam objectives.

Objective Map

Objective	Chapter
Section 1: Manage worksheets and workbooks	
1.1 Import data into workbooks	1
1.2 Navigate within workbooks	1
1.3 Format worksheets and workbooks	1, 2, 3, 4, 5
1.4 Customize options and views	1
1.5 Configure content for collaboration	1
Section 2: Manage data cells and ranges	
2.1 Manipulate data in worksheets	2
2.2 Format cells and ranges	1, 2
2.3 Define and reference named changes	2
2.4 Summarize data visually	2
Section 3: Manage tables and table data	
3.1 Create and format tables	3
3.2 Modify tables	1, 2, 3
3.3 Filter and sort table data	3
Section 4: Perform operations by using formulas and functions	
4.1 Insert references	4
4.2 Calculate and transform datas	4
4.3 Format and modify text	1, 2, 4
Section 5: Manage charts	
5.1 Create charts	5
5.2 Modify charts	5
5.3 Format charts	5

Assessment Test

1. What does the header row do in a table? (Choose all that apply.)
    A. It tells you what the columns are about.
    B. It allows you to sort data in a column.
    C. It sets apart the table from the rest of the worksheet.
    D. It allows you to filter data in a column.

2. When you copy a cell, what's the fastest way of copying it?
    A. Clicking Copy in the Home ribbon
    B. Right-clicking the cell and then clicking Copy in the context menu
    C. Pressing Ctrl+C
    D. Adding the Copy icon to the Quick Access Toolbar

3. What are ways in which you can identify data in a chart? (Choose all that apply.)
    A. Axes
    B. Legend
    C. Table
    D. Titles

4. What are the three reference types that you can add in a formula? (Choose all that apply.)
    A. Relative
    B. Absolute
    C. Numeric
    D. Mixed

5. What two types of files can you import into an Excel workbook? (Choose all that apply.)
    A. Word
    B. Text
    C. CSV
    D. PowerPoint

6. How can you select a chart element in your chart? (Choose all that apply.)
    A. Click the chart element.
    B. Click within the chart.
    C. Click the Chart Area box in the Format ribbon.
    D. Click Select Data in the Chart Design ribbon.

7. What option do you use to rotate text but not make the text itself change its orientation?

    A. Rotate Text Up

    B. Align Center

    C. Vertical Text

    D. Rotate Text Down

8. What does the SUM() function do?

    A. Adds all of the numbers in selected cells

    B. Summarizes the numbers in selected cells

    C. Calculates the average of all numbers in selected cells

    D. Counts all of the selected cells that have numbers in them

9. What drop-down list box do you select when you want to find information in an entire workbook?

    A. Search

    B. Look In

    C. Within

    D. Find What

10. What function do you use in a new cell to have Excel return the first few characters in a cell that contains text?

    A. MID()

    B. UPPER()

    C. LEN()

    D. LEFT()

11. What information can you show and hide in a table style? (Choose all that apply.)

    A. Header row

    B. First column

    C. Filter button

    D. Banded rows

12. Why would you assign a name to a range of cells?

    A. You don't have to because cells automatically have row numbers and column letters.

    B. You need to do this before you save the workbook.

    C. You can't find cells in a worksheet without naming them.

    D. You want to find groups of cells in a worksheet more easily.

13. What is the default row height in an Excel worksheet?

    A. 10 points

    B. 15 points

   C. One inch

   D. 72 points

14. How does the `COUNTA()` function differ from the `COUNT()` function?

   A. `COUNTA()` counts all the blank cells in a selected range.

   B. You can count specific numbers in the `COUNTA()` function.

   C. `COUNTA()` allows you to only count text, not numbers.

   D. The `COUNTA()` function counts selected cells that are not empty.

15. What does Excel call a chart created in a new worksheet?

   A. Chart sheet

   B. Chart1

   C. Whatever you decide the new worksheet should be

   D. Excel creates a new workbook and then you must give it a name.

16. When you need to sort table data with text and numbers in it, what is the best way to sort?

   A. In ascending order

   B. Using the sort and filter buttons in the header row

   C. A custom sort

   D. In descending order

17. What is a Sparkline chart?

   A. A chart format that lets you add graphic sparkles to your chart

   B. A small chart that quickly summarizes what you see in a row

   C. One of the built-in chart styles

   D. Another term for a win-loss chart

18. When would you use the `TEXTJOIN()` function instead of the `CONCAT()` function?

   A. When you want to ignore blank cells in the selected range

   B. You don't have to because `TEXTJOIN()` replaces `CONCAT()` in the latest version of Excel.

   C. To add a space between text in each cell

   D. When you don't want to type in the cell references within the formula

19. What does an error bar in a chart show? (Choose all that apply.)

   A. How inaccurate the data is in the chart

   B. Margins of error

   C. Standard deviation

   D. How much you can change the numeric value in a cell formula

20. When you format a table style, what formats can you change? (Choose all that apply.)

   A. Font

   B. Alignment

   C. Border

   D. Fill color and pattern

21. Your boss likes your chart but wants the background of the chart to be dark so that the text will stand out. How do you do this quickly?

   A. Apply a chart layout.

   B. Change the background color of the chart.

   C. Apply a different chart style.

   D. Tell your boss that there are no chart backgrounds other than white.

22. What are the minimum and maximum magnification views in a worksheet?

   A. 20 percent and 125 percent

   B. 10 percent and 150 percent

   C. 25 percent and 200 percent

   D. 5 percent and 300 percent

23. If you delete a row or column and immediately decide that you didn't want to do that, what do you do?

   A. Nothing

   B. Open the Home menu ribbon.

   C. Add the new row or column again.

   D. Press Ctrl+Z.

24. In the Paste Special dialog box, what button do you click to paste a number from one cell into a blank cell?

   A. Formats

   B. Values

   C. None

   D. Validation

25. What file formats can you save an Excel file to? (Choose all that apply.)

   A. XML

   B. Word

   C. PDF

   D. Excel

Answers to Assessment Test

1. B, D. Each cell in the header row contains a button that allows you to sort and filter data in the column. See Chapter 3 for more information.

2. C. Press Ctrl+C to copy all the information in one cell into an empty cell. See Chapter 2 for more information.

3. B, C. You can add a legend, a data table, as well as data labels to a chart to help you and others understand what the chart represents. See Chapter 5 for more information.

4. A, B, D. Excel can create relative, absolute, and mixed reference types in a cell formula. See Chapter 4 for more information.

5. B, C. You can import files with the TXT and CSV formats into an Excel workbook. See Chapter 1 for more information.

6. A, C. You can click on various elements within the chart. When you click the down arrow next to the Chart Area box in the Format ribbon, you see a drop-down list with all of the chart elements so that you can select an element easily. See Chapter 5 for more information.

7. C. When you click Vertical Text in the Orientation drop-down menu in the Home ribbon, Excel makes the text vertical, but it does not change the orientation so that each letter in the text appears in a separate line. See Chapter 2 for more information.

8. B. The SUM() function summarizes all selected cells that have numbers in them. See Chapter 4 for more information.

9. C. When you click the Within box, which shows the default Sheet option, a drop-down list appears so that you can select the Workbook option. See Chapter 1 for more information.

10. D. The LEFT() function tells Excel to read the first few characters of text and show that text in a new cell. See Chapter 4 for more information.

11. A, C. You can hide and show the header row in a table as well as filter buttons within a header row. See Chapter 3 for more information.

12. D. Naming a range of cells helps you find groups of cells in the same worksheet or a different worksheet in a workbook. See Chapter 2 for more information.

13. B. The default row height is 15 points. See Chapter 1 for more information.

14. D. The COUNTA() function counts cells in the selected range that are not empty, and the COUNT() function tells you how many cells have numbers. See Chapter 4 for more information.

15. A. You can move a chart to a separate worksheet, which Excel calls a chart sheet. See Chapter 5 for more information.

16. C. You need to create a custom sort so that you can decide if you want to sort first by text or by number. See Chapter 3 for more information.

17. B. A Sparkline chart summarizes all of the numerical data in other columns within a row. See Chapter 2 for more information.

18. C. The TEXTJOIN() function adds a delimiter of your choosing, including a space, between text in two or more cells that you combine with TEXTJOIN(). See Chapter 4 for more information.

19. B, C. An error bar can show both a margin of error and standard deviation. See Chapter 5 for more information.

20. A, C, D. You can change the font, border, and the fill color and/or pattern in the style. See Chapter 3 for more information.

21. C. Two of the built-in chart styles have dark backgrounds. See Chapter 5 for more information.

22. C. Excel has five magnification levels from 25 percent to 200 percent. See Chapter 1 for more information.

23. D. Press Ctrl+Z to bring back the deleted row or column and all of its data. See Chapter 3 for more information.

24. B. When you click the Values button in the Paste Special dialog box, you paste the value but not the formula from the copied cell into the blank cell. See Chapter 2 for more information.

25. A, C, D. You can save to XML, PDF, and Excel (with the extension .xlsx) versions. You can also save to older versions of Excel. See Chapter 1 for more information.

Chapter

1

Managing Worksheets and Workbooks

MICROSOFT EXAM OBJECTIVES COVERED IN THIS CHAPTER:

✓ **Manage worksheets and workbooks**

- Import data into workbooks
    - Import data from .txt files
    - Import data from .csv files
- Navigate within workbooks
    - Search for data within a workbook
    - Navigate to named cells, ranges, or workbook elements
    - Insert and remove hyperlinks
- Format worksheets and workbooks
    - Modify page setup
    - Adjust row height and column width
    - Customize headers and footers
- Customize options and views
    - Customize the Quick Access toolbar
    - Display and modify workbook content in different views
    - Freeze worksheet rows and columns
    - Change window views
    - Modify basic workbook properties
    - Display formulas
- Configure content for collaboration
    - Set a print area
    - Save workbooks in alternative file formats
    - Configure print settings
    - Inspect workbooks for issues

Welcome to this book, designed to help you study for and pass the MO-200 Microsoft Excel (Excel and Excel 2019) exam and become a certified Microsoft Office Specialist: Excel Associate. If you're all settled in, it's time to get this show on the road.

In this chapter, I'll start by showing you how to import data in other formats into Excel spreadsheets, which Excel calls *worksheets*, as well as collections of spreadsheets that Excel calls a *workbook*. Next, I'll show you how to navigate within a workbook and get comfortable with the Excel interface.

When you feel good about creating an Excel spreadsheet, I'll show you how to format that spreadsheet so that it looks the way you want. You'll also learn how to change the way information is presented to make Excel work better for you.

Finally, I'll show you how to get your spreadsheets ready to share in print and online. You'll also learn how to *inspect* your workbooks so that you can find and remove hidden properties as well as fix any issues with accessibility and compatibility.

I'll have an exercise at the end of every section in this chapter so that you can practice doing different tasks. Then, at the end of this chapter, you'll find a set of Review Questions that mimic the test questions you'll see on the MO-200 exam.

Importing Data into Workbooks

If you need to import existing data into a workbook, you should first check to see if the file is in a format that Excel likes. The most common formats are the native Excel, text, and *comma-delimited value (CSV)* formats.

The native Excel format has the .xls filename extension that dates all the way back to MS-DOS days, so you can obviously open those files. However, if you open an older XLS file, you may experience some issues with formatting.

It is more likely that you will receive files in text format with the .txt file extension and in comma-separated values (CSV) format with the .csv file extension. These two formats are what Microsoft focuses on in the MO-200 exam.

Text and CSV formats use a *delimiter*, which is a character that separates blocks of text, like between numbers. A text file will use a tab character to separate those blocks. A CSV file uses commas to separate each block of text.

After you open a text file, Excel does not change the format of the file. The file remains with the .txt or .csv extension as you save updates to it.

Excel allows you to import and export up to 1,048,576 rows and 16,384 columns of text from or to a TXT or CSV file.

Bringing in Data from TXT Files

When you receive a text file from someone else, check the file to ensure that it has a delimiter character. (If you don't see any, then you must decide whether to add the delimiter character or just return the text file to the sender and tell that person to fix the file.)

Once you are satisfied that the text file is ready for Excel, open the text file as follows:

1. Click the File menu option.
2. Click the Open menu option on the left side of the screen.
3. Click Browse.
4. In the Open dialog box, click All Excel Files in the lower-right area of the box.
5. Select Text Files from the drop-down list.
6. Navigate to the location that created the text file.
7. Click the text filename.
8. Click Open.

The Text Import Wizard dialog box opens (see Figure 1.1) and shows you what the text file looks like in step 1 of the wizard. Click the Next button to see what the text will look like in an Excel worksheet, and then click Next again to see the data format Excel assigns to each column.

FIGURE 1.1   Text Import Wizard dialog box

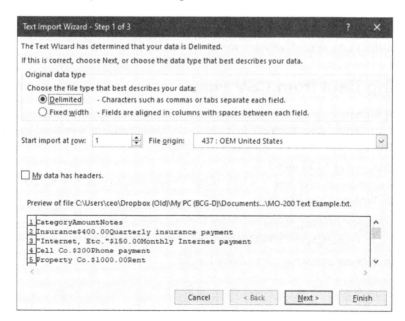

Though you can make changes in each of these steps, you don't need to know how to do that for the MO-200 exam. So, click the Finish button to view the imported spreadsheet.

A Cautionary Note About Formatting in a Text File

You see a yellow bar above the worksheet that cautions you about possible data loss if you save the worksheet in text format. Click Save As to save the file in another format (preferably Excel) or click Don't Show Again to hide this bar when you import other text files during the time you have Excel open. If you want to hide the bar but have it display the bar again if you import other text files, click the X icon at the right side of the bar.

Import a Text File into an Existing Worksheet

If you have text in another file that you want to place into a new worksheet within a workbook, here's how to do it:

1. Click the Data menu option.
2. If you see the Need To Import Data pop-up box, click Got It in the box.
3. In the Get & Transform Data section in the Data ribbon, as seen in Figure 1.2, click the From Text/CSV icon.
4. In the Import Data dialog box, navigate to the folder that contains the file.
5. Select the filename in the list.
6. Click Import.

The preview dialog box opens and shows you how the text will appear in the file. Click Load to import the data into a new worksheet with the name Sheet1, as you can see in the list of spreadsheet tabs at the bottom of the Excel window.

Importing Data from CSV Files

A CSV file is formatted specifically to be imported into spreadsheet software, and Excel knows CSV formatting cold. Each cell in a row is on one line of text separated by a comma with no spaces before or after the comma. For example:

> Title,Column 1,Column 2
> Excel considers each line in a CSV file to be one row, so you may have a
> CSV file that looks like this:

> Date,Payee,Amount,Notes
> 10/1,InsuranceCo,$400.00,Quarterly insurance payment

A comma does not appear at the end of a line.

FIGURE 1.2   Get & Transform section

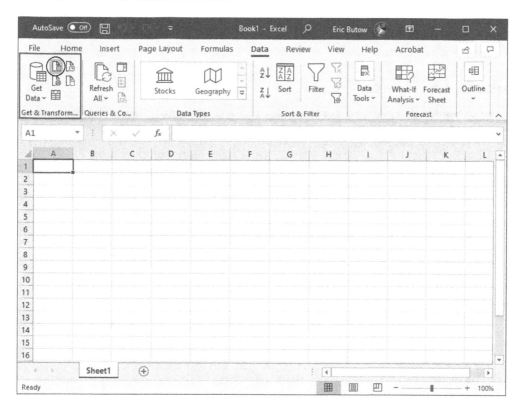

    What do you do when you have text that includes a comma in it? Put the text into quotes, and then add a comma outside the quote to start a new cell. For example, use **"One, Two",3,5** to add three separate cells in the row.

Add a CSV format file by following these steps:

1. Click the File menu option.
2. Click the Open menu option on the left side of the screen.
3. Click Browse.
4. In the Open dialog box, click All Excel Files in the lower-right area of the box.
5. Select Text Files from the drop-down list.
6. Navigate to the location that created the text file.
7. Click the text filename.
8. Click Open.

The Text Import Wizard dialog box opens (see Figure 1.3) and shows you what the text file looks like in step 1 of the wizard. Click the Next button to see what the text will look like in an Excel worksheet, and then click Next again to see the data format that Excel assigns to each column.

FIGURE 1.3 Import Data dialog box

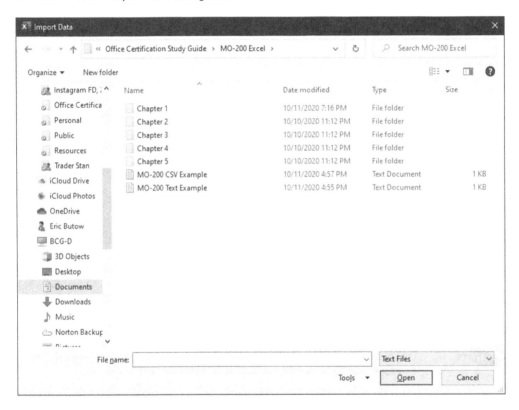

Insert a CSV File into a New Worksheet

You can also add a CSV file into a new worksheet within a workbook, much as you did with a text file, as follows:

1. Click the Data menu option.

2. If you see the Need To Import Data pop-up box, click Got It in the box.

3. In the Get & Transform Data section in the Data ribbon (see Figure 1.2), click the From Text/CSV icon.

4. In the Import Data dialog box (see Figure 1.3), navigate to the folder that contains the CSV file.

5. Click the filename in the list.

6. Click Import.

The preview dialog box appears, as shown in Figure 1.4, and it shows you how the text will appear in the file. Click Load to import the data into a new worksheet with the name Sheet1, as you can see in the list of spreadsheet tabs at the bottom of the Excel window.

FIGURE 1.4 Preview dialog box

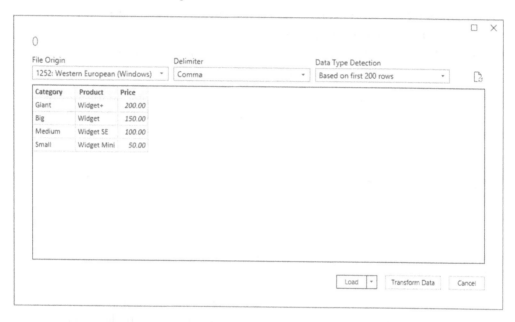

File Origin	Delimiter	Data Type Detection
1252: Western European (Windows)	Comma	Based on first 200 rows

Category	Product	Price
Giant	Widget+	200.00
Big	Widget	150.00
Medium	Widget SE	100.00
Small	Widget Mini	50.00

Load   Transform Data   Cancel

EXERCISE 1.1

Importing Text and CSV Format Files

1. Open a new workbook in Excel.

2. Import a text file into the workbook.

3. Import a CSV file into the workbook.

4. Save the workbook by pressing Ctrl+S.

Navigating Within Workbooks

After you populate a workbook, it can seem daunting to try to find the data within it. Excel has tools that make it easy.

Click the Search box in the Excel title bar, and then type the text that you want to find.

Searching for Data Within a Workbook

You can search for data on any worksheet in a workbook by following these steps:

1. Click the Home menu option, if necessary.

2. In the Editing section in the Home ribbon, click the Find & Select icon.

3. Select Find from the drop-down menu.

The Find And Replace dialog box appears so that you can search for information or replace one or more search terms, including specific formatting, with new text and/or formatting. If you want to replace text, select the Replace tab.

 You can also open the Find And Replace dialog box by pressing Ctrl+F. If you want to open the dialog box with the Replace tab active, press Ctrl+H.

Now you can replace text by typing the text you want to replace in the Find What text box, and then typing the replacement text in the Replace With text box.

Before you find and/or replace text, you may need to specify more information about what you want to find and/or replace. For example, you may want to change not only text in a cell, but also change the font and alignment of that text.

Open all find and replace options by clicking Options in the dialog box. The Find And Replace dialog box expands (see Figure 1.5) so that you can click one of the buttons or boxes to change information, as follows:

FIGURE 1.5   Find And Replace dialog box

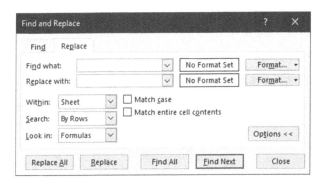

No Format Set   Informs you that no formatting has been applied to the text that you want to find and/or replace. If you change the format, the text in this button changes to Preview so that you can see how the text looks in the worksheet.

Format   Click the button to open the Find Format dialog box and change the format in one of six areas: Number, Alignment, Font, Border, Fill, and Protection. You will learn more about formatting cells later in this chapter.

Match Case   Find text that has the same case as what you typed in the Find box, such as a capitalized first letter in a word.

Match Entire Cell Contents   Find text that appears exactly like what you have typed in the Find box.

Within   The default selection in the Within box is Sheet, which searches for the text in the currently open worksheet. Click Sheet to select from the worksheet or the entire workbook in the drop-down list.

Search   The default selection in the Search box is By Rows, which searches for all instances of the search text in all rows. If you want to search for all instances of the text in all columns, click By Rows and then click By Columns in the drop-down list.

Look In   The Look In box has Formulas selected by default, which means that Excel will look for the search term in a specific type of text within the worksheet. If you have the Find tab open, then you can choose from Formulas, Values, Notes, or Comments in the drop-down list. If you have the Replace tab open, you can only select Formulas.

When you're ready to search for the text that you typed in the Find What text box, click the Find Next button to go to the next instance of the text in the open worksheet. If you search in the entire workbook, Excel searches for the text in the open worksheet first, and then it proceeds to search for all other instances of the text in subsequent worksheets.

If you click Find All, a dialog box appears that lists every instance of the text that Excel found in the worksheet or in the entire workbook. Click the instance in the list to open the cell in the corresponding worksheet.

Click Replace to replace only the next instance of the text with your replacement. If you want to replace any other text that meets your criteria, click the Replace button again to go to the next instance and replace that.

Replace all instances of the text and/or formatting in the Find text box by clicking the Replace All button. When Excel completes its search, a dialog box appears in the middle of the screen and tells you how many changes it made. Close the dialog box by clicking OK.

Important Search Tips

Unlike Microsoft Word, Excel allows you to add *wildcard* characters in the Find What box. Here's how:

- Add the question mark (?) to find a single character, such as **th?n** to find the words than, then, and thin.

- Add the asterisk (*) to find all characters that appear before or after a character, or between two characters. For example, type **d*r** to find dollar, divisor, and door.

- Add a tilde (~) before a question mark, asterisk, or another tilde to find cells that include a question mark, asterisk, or a tilde. For example, if you search for **Comment~?**, Excel shows all cells that have the text *Comment?*.

Navigating to Named Cells, Ranges, or Workbook Elements

Excel allows you to define names for a specific cell or for a *range* of cells, such as a block of income for a specific month. Here's how:

1. Select several cells by clicking and holding on one cell, then dragging the mouse pointer until all cells in the worksheet are highlighted, and then releasing the mouse button.

2. Click the Formulas menu option.

3. In the Defined Names section in the Formulas ribbon, as shown in Figure 1.6, click Define Name. (If the Excel window width is small, click the Define Name icon in the ribbon and then select Define Name from the drop-down menu.)

4. In the New Name dialog box, press Backspace and then type the new name in the Name box.

5. Click OK.

Now that you named a cell, go to another location in your worksheet or another worksheet in the workbook. You can find that named range by following these steps:

1. Click the Home menu option, if necessary.

2. Click Find And Select in the Editing section in the Home ribbon. (If the Excel window width is small, click the Editing icon in the ribbon and then click the Find And Select icon.)

3. From the drop-down menu, select Go To.

4. In the Go To dialog box, shown in Figure 1.7, click the name of the named range.

5. Click OK.

Excel highlights the named range within its worksheet.

A faster way to open the Go To dialog box is to press Ctrl+G.

FIGURE 1.6   The Define Name menu option

FIGURE 1.7   Go To dialog box

Inserting and Removing Hyperlinks

You can install as many *hyperlinks* as you want within the text of your workbook. After you insert a hyperlink, Excel gives you control over copying or moving a hyperlink, changing a hyperlink, and removing a hyperlink.

Start by clicking in the cell where you want to add the hyperlink, and then click the Insert menu option. In the Insert ribbon, click the Link icon, as seen in Figure 1.8. (If the Excel window width is small, click the Links icon in the ribbon and then click the Link icon.)

FIGURE 1.8   The Link icon

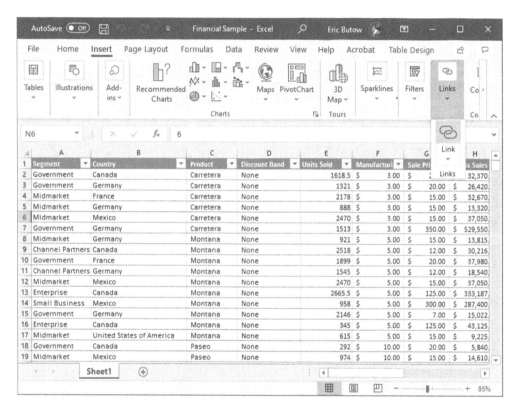

The Insert Hyperlink dialog box appears (see Figure 1.9) so that you can add your hyperlink.

You can add a hyperlink within the same worksheet, to another worksheet in your workbook, to another file or web page, or to an email address.

You can also open the Insert Hyperlink dialog box by pressing Ctrl+K.

FIGURE 1.9   The Insert Hyperlink dialog box

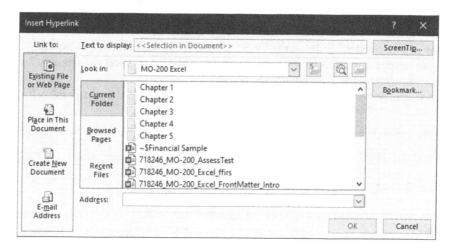

Within a Workbook

Adding a hyperlink to another location in a worksheet or workbook is useful when you need to move between cells quickly, and especially if you have long worksheets, many worksheets in a workbook, or both.

Start by clicking the cell and then opening the Insert Hyperlink dialog box. In the Link To box on the left side of the dialog box, click Place In This Document, as shown in Figure 1.10.

FIGURE 1.10   The Place In This Document menu option

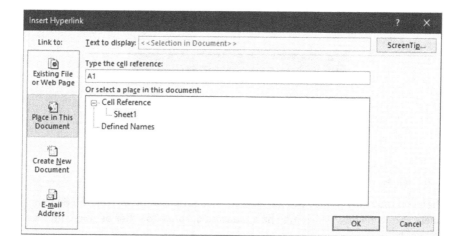

In the Type The Cell Reference text box, you can type the cell that you want to link to by typing the column letter and then the row number. For example, typing **C24** will link to the cell in column C, row 24.

If you want to link to a specific worksheet in your workbook, click the worksheet name under the Cell Reference header in the Or Select A Place In This Document list box.

You can select a named range by scrolling down in the list (if necessary) and then clicking the range name under the Defined Names header.

When you're done, click OK and the hyperlink appears within the text in the cell.

Give Your Readers Helpful Link Tips

You've been charged with creating a spreadsheet that will be sent not only to your boss, but also to senior leadership. You know that your workbook will have several worksheets, and you want to add links in cells that take people to different cells in the same worksheet and different worksheets. But how do you tell people what a link is all about when the link is in a cell that has a number in it?

Screen Tips to the rescue. When you add a *Screen Tip* to a link, a pop-up box appears when the user moves the mouse pointer over the link. Here's how to add a Screen Tip to a link:

1. Click the cell where you want to add the link.

2. Open the Insert Hyperlink dialog box, as you learned to do earlier in this section.

3. Click Screen Tip to the right of the Text To Display text box.

4. In the Set Hyperlink ScreenTip dialog box, type the text that you want to appear in the pop-up box.

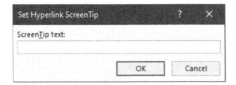

5. Click OK.

6. Close the Insert Hyperlink dialog box by clicking OK.

Now when you move the mouse pointer over the link for a second or two, the Screen Tip appears above the link, which may be a pleasant surprise to other people who view your workbook.

Link to an Existing File

You can add a hyperlink to another file, such as a Word file, that is important to your readers. When you link to another file, the appropriate program, such as Word, opens to view the linked file. Here's how to link to an existing file:

1. Click the cell where you want to add the hyperlink.
2. Click the Insert menu option.
3. In the Link section in the Insert ribbon, click the Link icon that you saw in Figure 1.8. (If the Excel window width is small, click the Links icon in the ribbon and then click the Link icon.)
4. In the Link To box on the left side of the dialog box, click Existing File Or Web Page, if necessary.
5. Click Current Folder (if necessary) or Recent Files to view the contents in the default Excel folder or all files that you have opened recently, respectively (see Figure 1.11).
6. Navigate to the folder that contains the file in the list, if necessary.
7. Click the file and then click OK.

FIGURE 1.11   A list of recently opened files

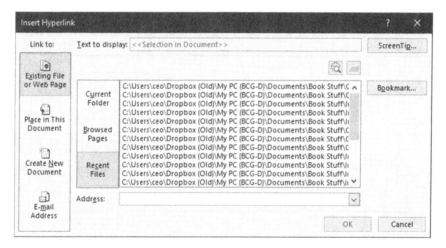

Link to a Web Page

You can add a hyperlink to a web page either on the web or on your network. That web page can be the home page, in which case you only need to type the URL of the site. If you need to link to a specific web page, you must type the full URL, including the web page name. You can also view recently browsed pages and select the page from the list.

When you link to a website, the default web browser opens and displays the page (or an error if the link is incorrect). Here's how to link to a web page:

1. Click the cell where you want to add the hyperlink.

2. Click the Insert menu option.

3. In the Link section in the Insert ribbon, click the Link icon that you saw in Figure 1.8. (If the Excel window width is small, click the Links icon in the ribbon and then click the Link icon.)

4. In the Link To box on the left side of the dialog box, click Existing File Or Web Page, if necessary.

5. Click Browsed Pages to view a list of all the web pages (see Figure 1.12).

6. Scroll up and down the list (if necessary), click the web page that you want to open, and then proceed to step 8.

7. If you don't see the web page that you want in the list, type the full URL in the Address box. That is, type **http://** or **https://** before the website and any specific web pages.

8. Click OK.

FIGURE 1.12   Browsed Pages list

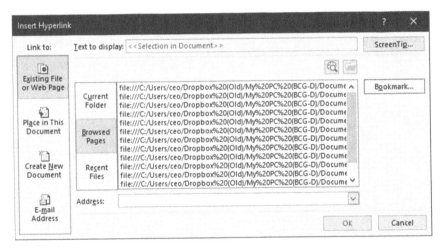

The link appears in the cell, and you can click the link to see if it opens the web page.

To an Email Address

Excel allows you to open a new email message so that you can send a message to that email address. You can also add a subject to the message. When you click the link, the default email program opens a new message window so that you can begin typing your message to the recipient.

Link to an email address by following these steps:

1. Click the cell where you want to add the hyperlink.

2. Click the Insert menu option.

3. In the Link section in the Insert ribbon, click the Link icon that you saw in Figure 1.8. (If the Excel window width is small, click the Links icon in the ribbon and then click the Link icon.)

4. In the Link To box on the left side of the Insert Hyperlink dialog box (see Figure 1.13), click E-mail Address.

5. Type the email address in the E-mail Address text box.

6. Add a subject for your message in the Subject text box.

7. Click OK.

FIGURE 1.13   E-mail Address menu option

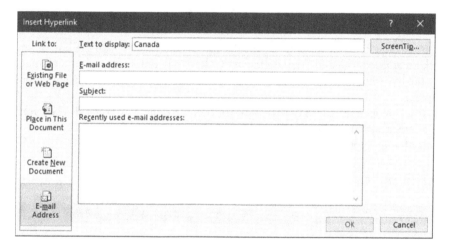

 If you type an email address in a cell, Excel adds a link to that email address automatically.

Copy and Move a Hyperlink

Once you create a hyperlink, you can copy it or move it to another cell. Here's how to do this:

1. Click the cell with the link that you want to move.

2. Click the Home menu option, if necessary.

3. Copy the cell with the link by clicking the Copy icon in the Clipboard section in the Home ribbon, and then proceed to step 5.

4. Move the cell with the link by clicking the Cut icon in the Clipboard section in the Home ribbon.

5. Click the cell in the workbook where you want to paste the text with the link.

6. Click the Paste icon in the Clipboard section in the Home ribbon.

 As in Word, you can copy the linked text within a cell by pressing Ctrl+C, cut the linked text from a cell by pressing Ctrl+X, and paste the text into a new cell by pressing Ctrl+V.

Change a Hyperlink

Excel allows you to change a hyperlink in a cell in one of three ways:

- You can change the destination of the link.

- You can change how the link appears in the cell.

- You can change the text in the cell and keep the link intact.

Start by clicking on a location in the cell that is outside the text with the link. If you can't, then click an adjacent cell and then use the arrow keys on your keyboard to highlight the cell with the hyperlink. (You will learn to change column widths and row height later in this chapter.)

Now you can open the Edit Hyperlink dialog box the same way you did when you inserted a hyperlink. The Edit Hyperlink dialog box appears (see Figure 1.14) and shows you the details of your hyperlink.

FIGURE 1.14 Edit Hyperlink dialog box

For example, if you link to an email address, then the E-mail Address option is selected in the Link To box, and you can see the email address and subject (if there is one) so that you can update that information quickly.

If you need to change the linked text that appears in the hyperlink, you can do so in the Text To Display box at the top of the dialog box.

When you finish making your changes, click OK. If you changed the link destination or email address, you may want to click the link to make sure that it works the way you expect.

You can change an existing hyperlink in your workbook by changing its destination, its appearance, or the text or graphic that is used to represent it.

Delete a Hyperlink

If you need to delete hyperlinked text in a cell, all you have to do is right-click the cell that has the link. In the context menu, as seen in Figure 1.15, click Remove Hyperlink. The link disappears from the text.

FIGURE 1.15   The Remove Hyperlink option in the context menu

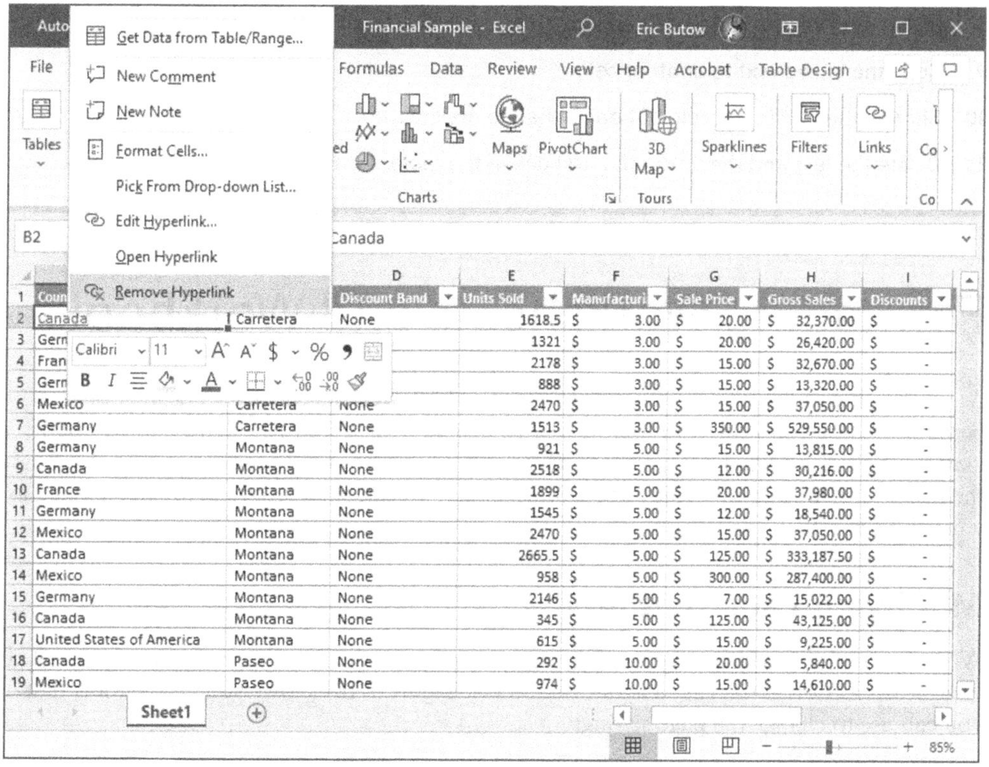

You can also delete the text in the cell as well as the link by right-clicking on the cell and then clicking Clear Contents in the context menu.

EXERCISE 1.2

Navigating in a Workbook

1. Open a new workbook.

2. Type text in 20 rows and 3 columns in the worksheet.

3. Select the 10 bottom rows and name the range.

4. Go to the top of the spreadsheet.

5. Search for the named range.

6. Click the first cell in the range.

7. Add text to the cell.

8. Link the text in the cell to a web page.

9. Copy the linked text to another cell.

10. Change the text in the cell, but don't change the link.

11. Delete the text and the link in the first cell in the table.

Formatting Worksheets and Workbooks

As you work with Excel, you may want to format how worksheets in a workbook appear, perhaps because you want it to look that way, people with whom you share the workbook expect it to look a certain way, or both. Excel allows you to modify the page settings, adjust the height of rows and the width of columns, and add headers and footers to pages, much as you would in a Word document.

Modifying Page Settings

When you need to modify page settings, begin by clicking the Page Layout menu option. The Page Setup section in the Page Layout ribbon (see Figure 1.16) shows you all the tools that you can use to change the page settings.

FIGURE 1.16   Page Setup section options

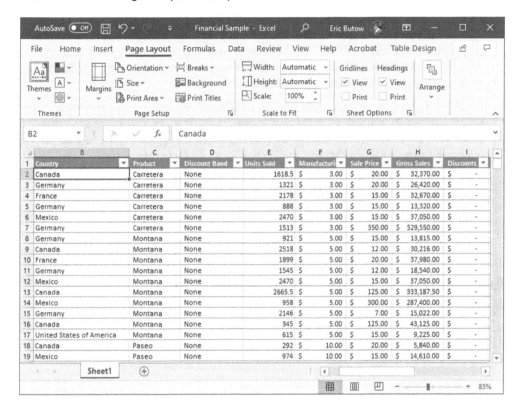

All of these icons appear in the ribbon no matter whether your window width is 800 pixels, as seen in Figure 1.16, or larger. Click one of the following options to make changes:

Margins   Change the margins for each printed page within a worksheet in the drop-down menu. The default is Normal, but you can select from Wide and Narrow margins. If none of the default options work for you, click Custom Margins at the bottom of the menu and then set your own margins in the Page Setup dialog box.

Orientation   Change between Portrait and Landscape orientation in the drop-down menu. The default is Portrait.

Size   Set the paper size in the drop-down menu. The default is Letter, which is 8.5 inches wide by 11 inches high. If none of the paper sizes meet your needs, click More Page Sizes at the bottom of the menu and then set your own paper size in the Page Setup dialog box.

Print Area   If you want to print a range of cells within a worksheet, select the cells by clicking and holding one cell in the range and then dragging until Excel selects all the cells. When you're done, release the mouse button and then click Print Area. From the drop-down list, select Set Print Area. You can remove the print area by clicking Print Area and then selecting Clear Print Area from the drop-down menu. You will learn more about setting a print area later in this chapter.

Breaks   Add a page break after the currently selected cell or row in your worksheet by selecting Insert Page Break from the drop-down menu. You can also remove the page break after the currently selected cell by clicking Remove Page Break. If you want to remove all page breaks in the workbook, click Reset All Page Breaks.

Background   Add a background image to your worksheet. You can add an image from a file on your computer, from the web using a Bing search, or from a OneDrive folder.

Print Titles   Opens the Page Setup dialog box so that you can tell Excel to print the same rows at the top and/or same columns at the left side of your printed worksheet.

Adjusting Row Height and Column Width

Excel has default row heights and column widths, but you may have to change those for readability. For example, you may need to extend the column width so that you can see all of the text in a cell within that column. The minimum, default, and maximum heights for rows and columns are as follows:

Minimum height, rows, and columns: 0 points

Default row height: 15 points

Default column width: 8.43 points

Maximum row height: 409 points

Maximum column width: 255 points

     There are 72 points in an inch, or 2.54 centimeters.

Set Column to Specific Width

Here's how to change the column width:

1.   Select a cell in the column.

2.   Click the Home menu option, if necessary.

3. In the Cells section in the Home ribbon, click the Format icon. If your Excel window width is smaller, as shown in Figure 1.17, click the Cells icon and then click the Format icon.

4. Select Column Width from the drop-down menu, as shown in Figure 1.17.

5. In the Column Width dialog box, press the Backspace key to delete the highlighted measurement.

6. Type the new width in points.

7. Click OK.

FIGURE 1.17 Column Width option

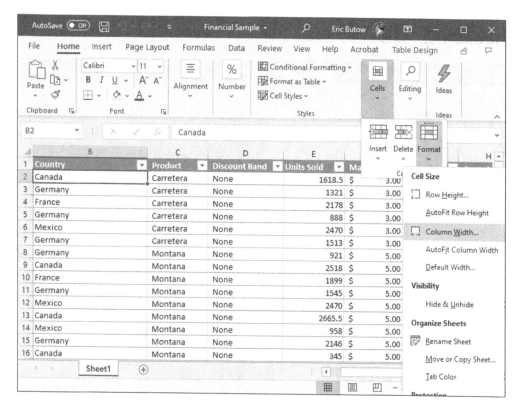

 You can also open the Column Width dialog box by right-clicking the column letter in the heading above the worksheet and then selecting Column Width from the context menu.

Change the Column Width to Fit the Contents Automatically with AutoFit

Excel has a built-in AutoFit feature that allows you to fit the width of the contents automatically. AutoFit a column by following these steps:

1. Select a cell in the column.

2. Click the Home menu option, if necessary.

3. In the Cells section in the Home ribbon, click the Format icon. If your Excel window width is smaller, as shown in Figure 1.18, click the Cells icon and then click the Format icon.

4. Select AutoFit Column Width from the drop-down menu, as shown in Figure 1.18.

FIGURE 1.18 AutoFit Column Width option

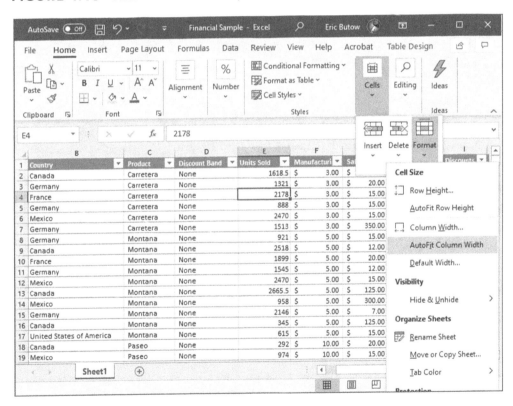

The column width changes to accommodate the text in the cell with the longest width.

Match the Column Width to Another Column

If you want more than one column to have the same width, here's how to do that:

1. Click a cell within the column that has your preferred width.

2. Click the Home menu option, if necessary.

3. In the Clipboard section in the Home ribbon, click Copy.

4. Click a cell in the column to which you want to apply the width.

5. In the Clipboard section in the Home ribbon, click the down arrow under the Paste icon.

6. Click the Keep Source Column Widths icon in the drop-down menu, as shown in Figure 1.19.

FIGURE 1.19   Keep Source Column Widths icon

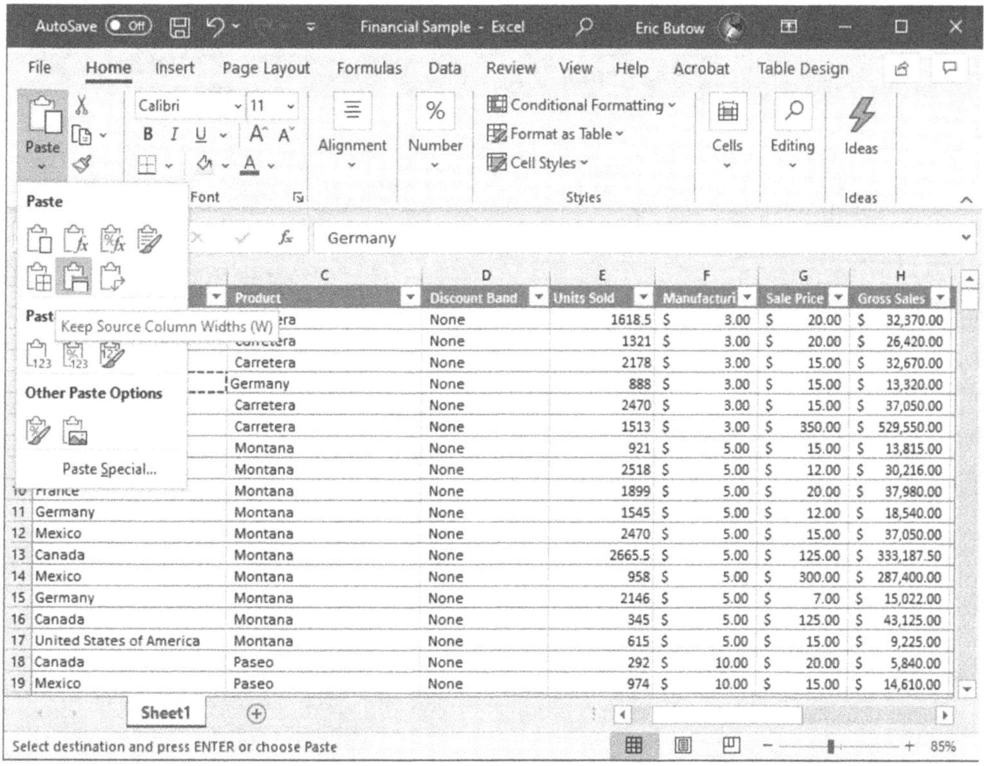

When you move the mouse pointer over the icon, the column width changes automatically so that you can preview the width of the column before you click the icon. If you move the mouse pointer away from the icon, the column reverts to its previous width.

Change the Default Width for All Columns on a Worksheet

If all you need is one width for all columns within a worksheet, change the default width by following these steps:

1. Click the Home menu option, if necessary.

2. In the Cells section in the Home ribbon, click Format. If the width of your Excel window is smaller, click the Cells icon and then click Format.

3. Select Default Width from the drop-down menu, as shown in Figure 1.20.

4. In the Standard Width dialog box, press Backspace to delete the width in the Standard Column Width text box.

5. Type the new width in points.

6. Click OK.

FIGURE 1.20 Default Width option

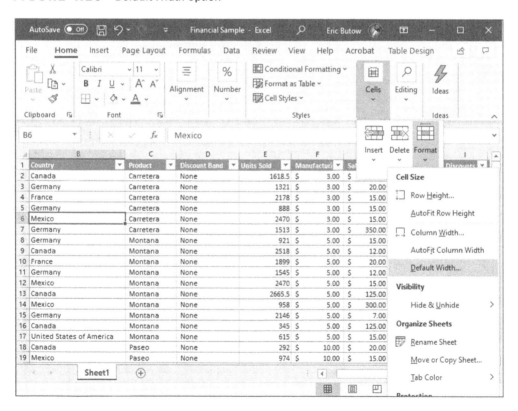

Excel resizes all columns in the worksheet to the width you specified.

Change the Width of Columns by Using the Mouse

When you want to change the width of a column by using the mouse, move the mouse pointer to the right border of the column heading above the worksheet. The cursor changes to a double-headed arrow, as shown in Figure 1.21.

FIGURE 1.21   The resize mouse pointer between two column headings

	A	B	C	D	E	F	G	H
1	Segment	Country	Product	Discount Band	Units Sold	Manufacturi	Sale Price	Gross Sales
2	Government	Canada	Carretera	None	1618.5	$ 3.00	$ 20.00	$ 32,370
3	Government	Germany	Carretera	None	1321	$ 3.00	$ 20.00	$ 26,420
4	Midmarket	France	Carretera	None	2178	$ 3.00	$ 15.00	$ 32,670
5	Midmarket	Germany	Carretera	None	888	$ 3.00	$ 15.00	$ 13,320
6	Midmarket	Mexico	Carretera	None	2470	$ 3.00	$ 15.00	$ 37,050
7	Government	Germany	Carretera	None	1513	$ 3.00	$ 350.00	$ 529,550
8	Midmarket	Germany	Montana	None	921	$ 5.00	$ 15.00	$ 13,815
9	Channel Partners	Canada	Montana	None	2518	$ 5.00	$ 12.00	$ 30,216
10	Government	France	Montana	None	1899	$ 5.00	$ 20.00	$ 37,980
11	Channel Partners	Germany	Montana	None	1545	$ 5.00	$ 12.00	$ 18,540
12	Midmarket	Mexico	Montana	None	2470	$ 5.00	$ 15.00	$ 37,050
13	Enterprise	Canada	Montana	None	2665.5	$ 5.00	$ 125.00	$ 333,187
14	Small Business	Mexico	Montana	None	958	$ 5.00	$ 300.00	$ 287,400
15	Government	Germany	Montana	None	2146	$ 5.00	$ 7.00	$ 15,022
16	Enterprise	Canada	Montana	None	345	$ 5.00	$ 125.00	$ 43,125
17	Midmarket	United States of America	Montana	None	615	$ 5.00	$ 15.00	$ 9,225
18	Government	Canada	Paseo	None	292	$ 10.00	$ 20.00	$ 5,840
19	Midmarket	Mexico	Paseo	None	974	$ 10.00	$ 15.00	$ 14,610

Now you can click, hold, and drag the boundary of the column heading to the left or right. As you drag, the width of the column to the left of the pointer changes, and a pop-up box above the pointer shows you the exact width of the column. When the column is the size that you want, release the mouse button.

NOTE   You can automatically fit a column to the width of the text inside it by moving the mouse pointer to the border on the right side of the column header and then double-clicking on the border.

Set a Row to a Specific Height

When you want to set a row to a specific height, the process for doing so is much the same as setting a column to a specific width, as follows:

1. Select a cell in the row.

2. Click the Home menu option, if necessary.

3. In the Cells section in the Home ribbon, click the Format icon. If your Excel window width is smaller, as shown in Figure 1.22, click the Cells icon and then click the Format icon.

4. Select Row Height from the drop-down menu, as shown in Figure 1.22.

5. In the Row Height dialog box, press the Backspace key to delete the highlighted measurement.

6. Type the new height in points.

7. Click OK.

Excel resizes the row and vertically aligns the text at the bottom of the cells in the row.

FIGURE 1.22   Row Height option

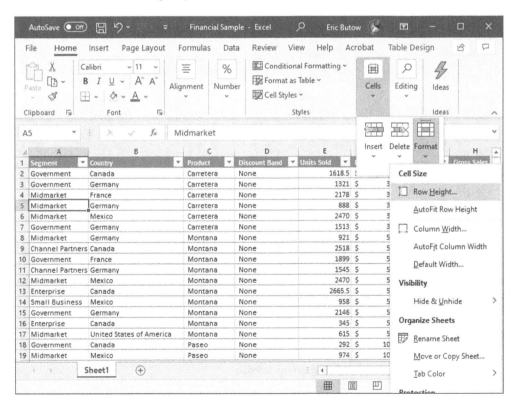

You can also open the Column Width dialog box by right-clicking the row number to the left of the worksheet and then selecting Row Height from the context menu.

Change the Row Height to Fit the Contents with AutoFit

As with columns, the built-in AutoFit feature allows you to fit the height of rows automatically to match the largest height in a row. Here's how to do this:

1. Select a cell in the row.
2. Click the Home menu option, if necessary.
3. In the Cells section in the Home ribbon, click the Format icon. If your Excel window width is smaller, as shown in Figure 1.23, click the Cells icon and then click the Format icon.
4. Select AutoFit Row Height from the drop-down menu, as shown in Figure 1.23.

    The row height changes to accommodate the text in the cell with the largest height.

FIGURE 1.23   AutoFit Row Height option

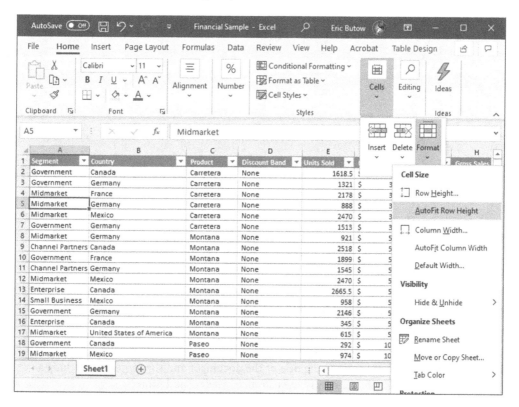

Change the Height of Rows by Using the Mouse

You can change the height of a row more quickly by using the mouse. Start by moving the mouse pointer to the bottom border of the row heading to the left of the worksheet. The cursor changes to a double-headed arrow, as shown in Figure 1.24.

FIGURE 1.24 The resize mouse pointer between two row headings

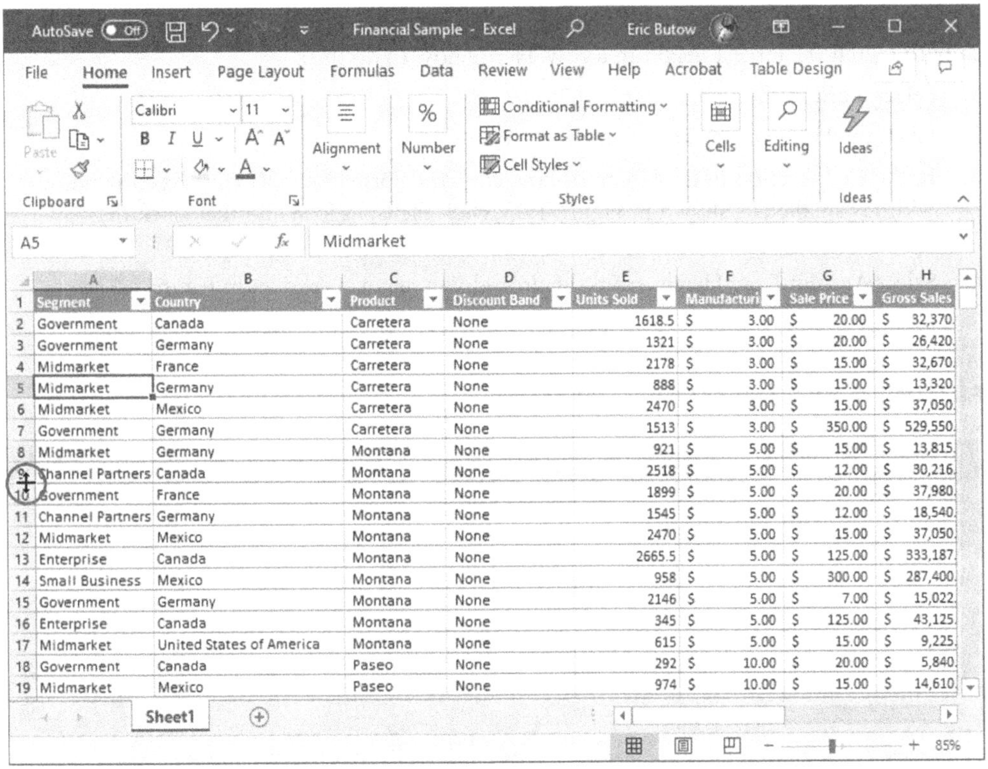

Now you can click, hold, and drag the boundary of the row heading up and down. As you drag, the height of the row above the pointer changes, and a pop-up box above the pointer shows you the exact height of the row. When the row is the size that you want, release the mouse button.

Customizing Headers and Footers

As with a Word document, you can add headers and footers into an Excel spreadsheet that will make it easier for users who view your documents in paper or PDF format to read it. For example, a header can include the title of the document and the footer can include a page number. Excel also makes it easy to customize headers and footers.

Add a Header or Footer

Add a header and footer into a worksheet by clicking the Insert menu option. In the Text section in the Insert menu ribbon, click the Header & Footer icon in the Text section (see Figure 1.25).

FIGURE 1.25 Header & Footer icon

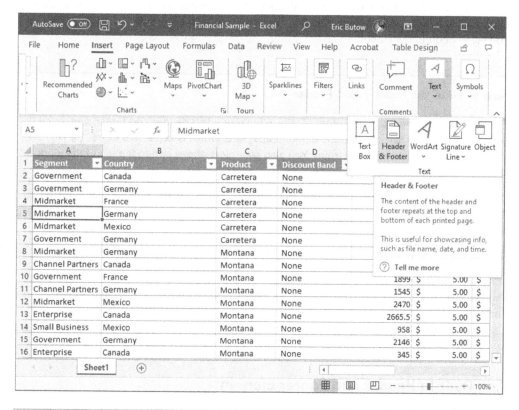

 If your Excel window has a small width, and you don't see the Text section, here's what to do:

1. Click the right arrow button at the right side of the ribbon to view the rest of the ribbon icons.
2. Click the Text icon.
3. Click the Header & Footer icon.

The worksheet appears in Page Layout view with the cursor blinking within the middle section of the header. The cursor is in the center position so that the text will be centered on the page.

Click the left section of the header to place the cursor so that it is left-aligned in that section. Click the right section of the header to place the cursor right-aligned in that header. The text in all three sections in the header are vertically aligned at the top.

The Header & Footer ribbon appears automatically so that you can add a footer by clicking the Go To Footer icon in the Navigation section. The footer section appears at the bottom of the spreadsheet page with the cursor blinking in the center section of the footer.

Like the Header section, the footer is divided into three sections, but the text in all three sections is vertically aligned at the bottom. You can return to the header by clicking the Go To Header icon in the ribbon.

How to Hide the Header and Footer

The Page Layout view appears automatically when you add a header and footer, and you'll notice that the page is laid out in the default paper size, which is Letter (8.5 inches by 11 inches), as well as the default margins. You also see rulers above and to the left of the worksheet as you would in a Word document.

If you want to return the worksheet view to the default Normal view, click anywhere inside the worksheet (but not in the header or footer). Click the View menu option, and then click Normal in the Workbook Views section in the View ribbon.

Note that when you return to Normal view, gray page separator dashes appear in the worksheet.

You can view the header again by clicking the Page Layout View icon in the View ribbon. Then you can edit the header or footer by clicking the appropriate section.

Add Built-In Header and Footer Elements

Excel contains a number (ahem) of features for adding header and footer elements so that you don't have to update them automatically, such as with a page number.

After you add a header or footer and you have clicked within a section, the Header & Footer ribbon appears. You can add built-in elements from the Header & Footer and the Header & Footer Elements sections.

Header & Footer Section

In the Header & Footer section in the ribbon, click the Header icon to view a list of built-in header elements that you can add (see Figure 1.26).

FIGURE 1.26 Header element drop-down list

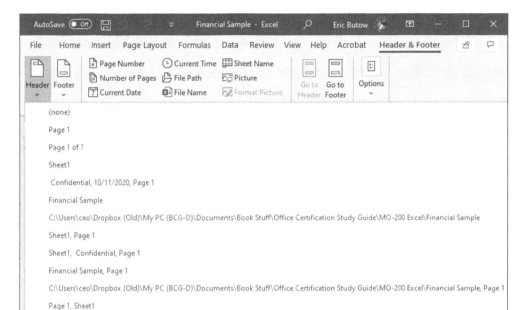

Some entries in the list have two or three options. An entry with two elements will place them in the header sections specified within the built-in entry. For example, the page number appears in the center section and the worksheet name appears in the right section.

After you select a header element from the drop-down list, Excel adds the header automatically and places the cursor back in the worksheet so that you can resume your work.

If you click within a footer, you can add a built-in footer element by clicking the Footer icon and then selecting a built-in footer element from the drop-down list. Once you do, Excel adds the footer and places the cursor in the worksheet.

Header & Footer Elements

The Header & Footer Elements section contains nine elements, as shown in Figure 1.27.

If you don't see the Header & Footer ribbon, click the Header & Footer menu option.

FIGURE 1.27   Header & Footer Elements section

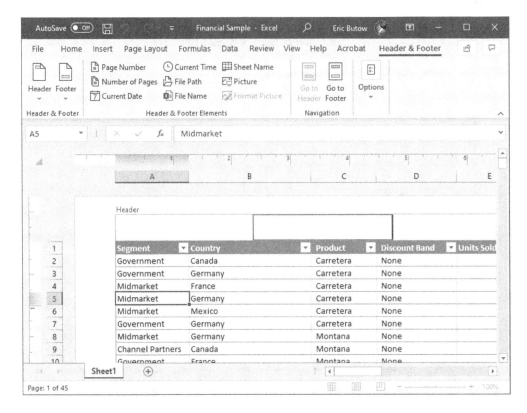

When you click one of the buttons (except for Format Picture, which is only active after you add a picture), its field name appears within brackets and preceded by an ampersand (&), such as &[Date]. Some fields are preceded by text, such as Page &[Page].

After you add the element and click outside the header or footer, the element appears properly. Click one of the icons in the ribbon to add the element.

Page Number   Adds the current page number in the worksheet

Number Of Pages   Displays the number of pages in the worksheet that contain data

Current Date   Displays the current date. Excel does not update the date until you click the date in the header or footer and then click in the worksheet again.

Current Time   Displays the current time. Excel updates the time when you click the time in the header or footer and then click in the worksheet.

Add the workbook folder path and file name   Add a page break after the currently selected cell or row in your worksheet by selecting Insert Page Break from the drop-down menu. You can also remove the page break after the currently selected cell by clicking Remove Page Break. If you want to remove all page breaks in the workbook, click Reset All Page Breaks.

Add the workbook file name   Add a background image to your worksheet. You can add an image from a file on your computer, from the web using a Bing search, or from a OneDrive folder.

Add the worksheet name   Opens the Page Setup dialog box so that you can tell Excel to print the same rows at the top and/or the same columns at the left side of your printed worksheet

Picture   Opens the Insert Pictures dialog box so that you can insert a picture from a file on your computer or network, from a Bing Image Search, or from your default One-Drive folder. If the picture is larger than the header or footer, the picture appears on the page within the left and right margins.

Format Picture   Opens the Format Picture dialog box so that you can change the size and orientation, crop the picture, change the color, brightness, and contrast settings, and add alternative (Alt) text

Delete a Header and Footer

If you need to delete the element, double-click the element name to select it, and then press Delete on the keyboard. The header and footer remain in the document, and the page separator dashes appear in the worksheet.

You can delete the header and footer from the entire workbook by following these steps:

1. Click the Page Layout menu option.
2. In the Page Setup section in the Page Layout ribbon, click Print Titles.
3. In the Page Setup dialog box, as shown in Figure 1.28, click the Header/Footer tab.
4. Click the header and/or footer name in the Header or Footer box, respectively.
5. Click (none) in the list. (You may need to scroll up and down in the list to find it.)
6. Click OK.

Even when you remove a header and/or footer, the header and footer place-holder remains in the document if you want to add a header or footer later.

You can view the header and footer again by clicking the View menu option, clicking the Page Layout icon in the Workbook Views section, and then clicking Add Header or Add Footer at the top and bottom of the page, respectively.

FIGURE 1.28   Page Setup dialog box

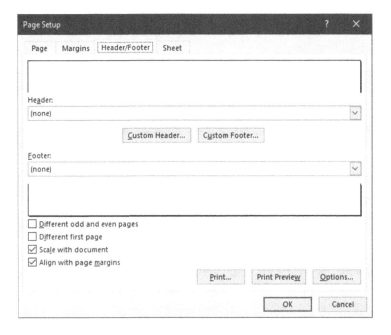

EXERCISE 1.3

Formatting a Workbook

1.   Open a new workbook.

2.   Change the column A width to 40 points.

3.   Increase the height of row 1 as you see fit by using the mouse.

4.   Add a header with the current date.

5.   Add a footer with the page number.

6.   Return to the normal workbook view and continue working in your worksheet.

Customizing Options and Views

Excel offers you plenty of ways to change the options that you can access as you work in a workbook, as well as what you see in ribbons and toolbars so that you can get your work done more quickly.

You can customize the Quick Access Toolbar, create and modify custom views, and freeze rows and columns in a worksheet so that they don't move as you navigate within a worksheet.

Customizing the Quick Access Toolbar

Excel includes a toolbar for accessing tools and commands quickly without having to click the menu option and then find the option in the ribbon. Microsoft naturally calls this the Quick Access Toolbar, and you can add features from a ribbon to the toolbar.

The toolbar itself appears at the left side of the Excel window title bar, but you can move the toolbar below the ribbon instead. By default, there are only four commands that you can access in the toolbar:

- You can turn the AutoSave feature off and on; the default setting is off.
- Save
- Undo
- Redo

 As you use the Quick Access Toolbar, keep the following in mind:

- You can only add commands and tools to the toolbar, not other things that you may want to add quickly, such as cell styles.
- The toolbar only appears on one line. If there are more icons in the toolbar than it can hold, then you will see a right arrow at the right side of the toolbar that you can click to view more icons.
- The button sizes in the toolbar are fixed.

Add a Command to the Quick Access Toolbar

You can add a command to the toolbar in one of two ways. The first is to add the command from a ribbon. The other is to add a command from the Customize Quick Access Toolbar menu.

Add from the Ribbon

Whenever you're in a ribbon and you see an option that you want to add to the Quick Access Toolbar, here's what to do:

1. Click the menu option to open its associated ribbon.
2. In the ribbon, right-click the word or icon associated with the command that you want to add to the toolbar.
3. Select Add To Quick Access Toolbar from the drop-down menu (see Figure 1.29).

You see the new icon at the right side of the toolbar, as you can also see in Figure 1.29.

FIGURE 1.29 The new icon in the Quick Access Toolbar

◢	A	B	C	D	E	F
1	Segment ▼	Country ▼	Product ▼	Discount Band ▼	Units Sold ▼	Manufacturi ▼ Sal◄
2	Government	Canada	Carretera	None	1618.5	$ 3.00 $
3	Government	Germany	Carretera	None	1321	$ 3.00 $
4	Midmarket	France	Carretera	None	2178	$ 3.00 $
5	Midmarket	Germany	Carretera	None	888	$ 3.00 $
6	Midmarket	Mexico	Carretera	None	2470	$ 3.00 $
7	Government	Germany	Carretera	None	1513	$ 3.00 $
8	Midmarket	Germany	Montana	None	921	$ 5.00 $
9	Channel Partners	Canada	Montana	None	2518	$ 5.00 $
10	Government	France	Montana	None	1899	$ 5.00 $
11	Channel Partners	Germany	Montana	None	1545	$ 5.00 $
12	Midmarket	Mexico	Montana	None	2470	$ 5.00 $
13	Enterprise	Canada	Montana	None	2665.5	$ 5.00 $
14	Small Business	Mexico	Montana	None	958	$ 5.00 $
15	Government	Germany	Montana	None	2146	$ 5.00 $
16	Enterprise	Canada	Montana	None	345	$ 5.00 $

Add from the Customize Quick Access Toolbar Menu

You can also add a command from the Customize Quick Access Toolbar drop-down menu. Start by clicking the down arrow at the right side of the Quick Access Toolbar in the Excel window title bar. If you haven't added any icons to the toolbar, you will see the icon to the right of the Redo icon.

Next, click one of the options without a check mark to the left of the command name in the drop-down menu, as you can see in Figure 1.30. (You will learn how to remove options from the toolbar later in this chapter.)

If you want to see a list of all commands and add them to the Quick Access Toolbar, select More Commands from the drop-down menu to open the Excel Options dialog box. Using this dialog box to add commands is (mostly) beyond the scope of this book, but you can explore this dialog box at your leisure.

FIGURE 1.30 Customize Quick Access Toolbar drop-down menu

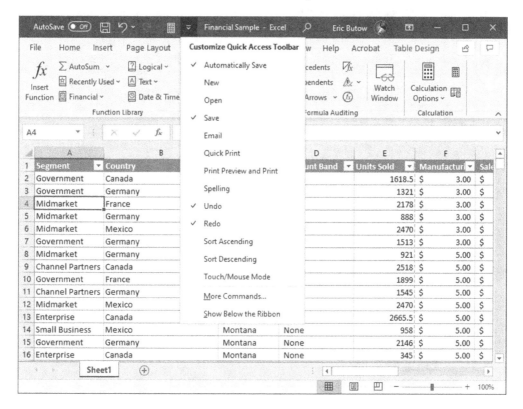

Remove a Command from the Quick Access Toolbar

There are two ways that you can remove a command from the Quick Access Toolbar:

- Right-click the command in the toolbar, and then select Remove From Quick Access Toolbar from the drop-down menu.
- Click the down arrow at the right side of the Quick Access Toolbar, and then click a command that has a check mark next to it.

In both cases, the icon disappears from the toolbar and you can go back to work.

Move the Quick Access Toolbar

By default, the Quick Access Toolbar appears within the Excel window title bar. You can move the toolbar below the ribbon, where it will stay even if you close Excel and reopen it.

All you need to do to move the Quick Access Toolbar is click the down arrow at the right side of the toolbar and then click Show Below The Ribbon. The toolbar appears under the ribbon (see Figure 1.31).

FIGURE 1.31   The Quick Access Toolbar below the ribbon

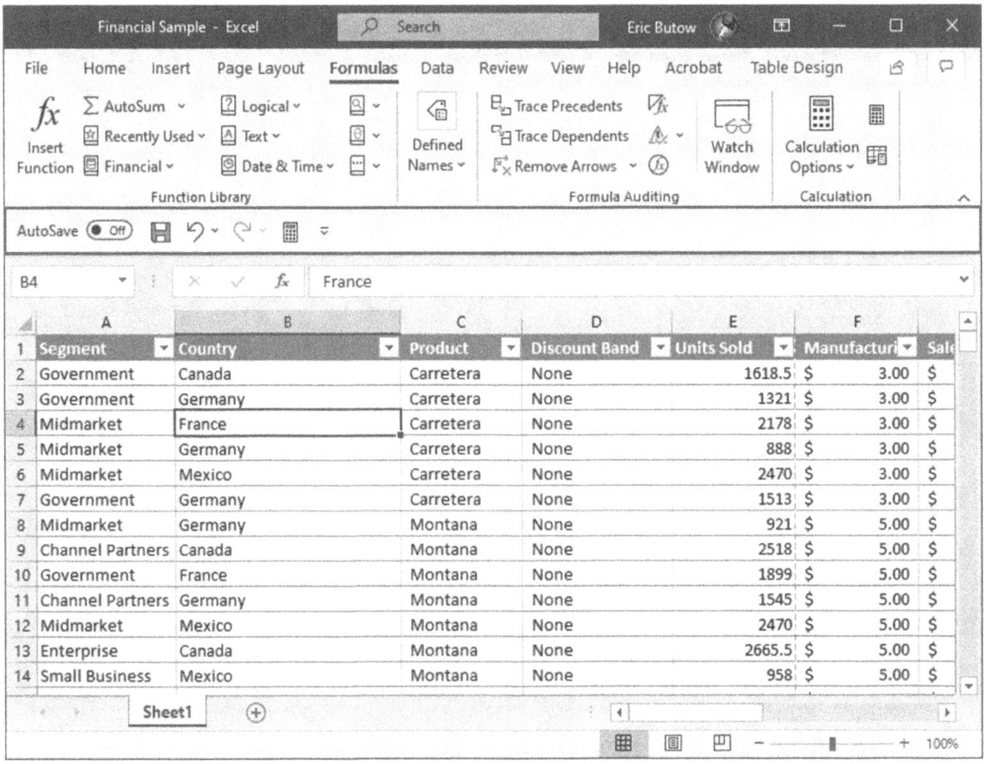

If you want to move the toolbar back, click the down arrow at the right side of the toolbar and then select Show Above The Ribbon from the drop-down menu.

Reset the Quick Access Toolbar to the Default Settings

Follow these steps if you need to reset the Quick Access Toolbar to its default settings:

1. Click the down arrow at the right side of the Quick Access Toolbar.
2. Select More Commands from the drop-down menu.
3. Click Reset in the Excel Options dialog box, as shown in Figure 1.32.
4. Select Reset Only Quick Access Toolbar from the drop-down menu.
5. Click Yes in the Reset Customizations dialog box.
6. Click OK.

All of the commands that you added in the toolbar disappear, and you see only the four default options.

FIGURE 1.32 Reset button in Excel Options dialog box

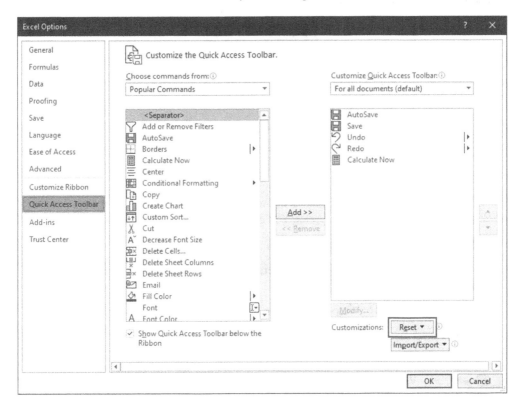

Displaying and Modifying Workbook Content in Different Views

Excel allows you to change the view on the document so that you can zoom in and zoom out within a worksheet, but Excel only has five built-in magnification levels, from 25 percent to 200 percent, as well as the ability to fit the worksheet to the window.

What's more, you can set your own custom view type. Here's how:

1. Click the View menu option.
2. In the Zoom section in the View ribbon, click the Zoom icon.
3. In the Zoom dialog box, as shown in Figure 1.33, select the custom view or type it in the Custom box. The default custom setting is 100 percent.
4. Click OK.

FIGURE 1.33   Zoom dialog box

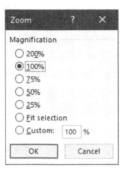

When you view your document, Excel allows you to create a custom view to make workbook content appear the way you prefer. You can save three different types of views:

Display settings: Used to hide rows, columns, and filter settings

Print settings: Used to set margins, headers, footers, and other worksheet and page settings

A specific print area: Settings applied to a particular print area

You can also create multiple views, each with a different name.

When you add a custom view, keep the following in mind:

- You can only add a custom view to a worksheet that you added within that one worksheet. If you create a different worksheet in the same workbook or a new one, you need to create new custom views for that worksheet.
- If any worksheet in the workbook contains an Excel table, which you will learn about in Chapter 3, "Working with Tables and Table Data," then Custom Views is disabled.

Create a Custom View

Here's how to create a custom view in a worksheet:

1. Click the View menu option.
2. In the Workbook Views section in the View ribbon, click the Custom Views icon (see Figure 1.34).
3. In the Custom Views dialog box, click Add.
4. In the Add View dialog box, as shown in Figure 1.35, type the name for the view in the Name box.

FIGURE 1.34   Custom Views icon

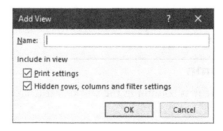

5.   The two view settings are selected by default so that you will view print settings as well as hidden row, column, and filter settings. Turn one or both views off by clicking the appropriate check box.

6.   Click OK.

FIGURE 1.35   Add View dialog box

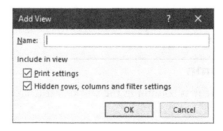

Apply a Custom View

When you want to show a view, open the Custom Views dialog box again. You see the view highlighted in the list, as seen in Figure 1.36. (If you have more views than the window can hold, scroll up and down in the list to find it.) Click the view name in the list, if necessary, and then click Show.

FIGURE 1.36   The selected view in the list is at the top.

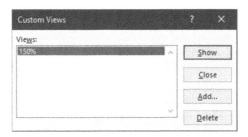

You see the changes in your view. For example, if your custom view is 150 percent, the view of your worksheet changes to 150 percent of the default magnification.

Delete a Custom View

When you want to delete a custom view, follow these steps:

1. Open the Custom Views dialog box, as you learned to do earlier in this chapter.
2. In the Custom Views dialog box, click the view that you want to delete in the list.
3. Click Delete.
4. Click Yes in the dialog box.

The view disappears from the list. Close the dialog box by clicking Close.

Freezing Worksheet Rows and Columns

You can freeze a row or column in a worksheet so that a row and/or column remains visible on the worksheet even as you scroll through it. This feature is especially useful if you have header rows or columns to which you will need to refer as you scroll through a worksheet that doesn't fit in the Excel window.

Freeze the First Column

If you only want to freeze the first column in the worksheet (that is, column A), follow these steps:

1. Click the View menu option.
2. In the Window section, click Freeze Panes.
3. Select Freeze First Column from the drop-down menu, as shown in Figure 1.37.

FIGURE 1.37   Freeze Panes drop-down menu

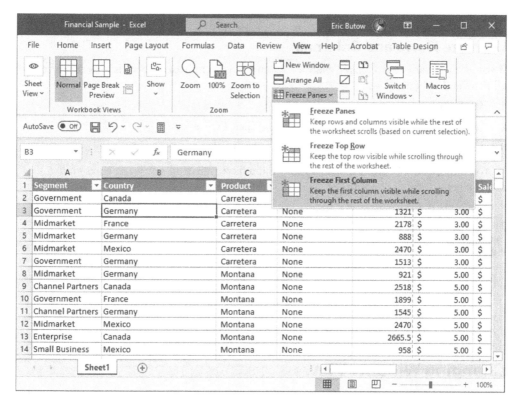

A darker line appears at the right edge of column A, which shows you that the column is frozen.

Freeze the First Row

If you want to freeze only the first row in the worksheet (that is, row 1), follow these steps:

1. Click the View menu option.
2. In the Window section in the View ribbon, click Freeze Panes.
3. Select Freeze Top Row from the drop-down menu in Figure 1.37.

A darker line appears at the right edge of row 1, which shows you that the row is frozen.

Freeze Any Column or Row

You can select one or more columns or rows to freeze. However, you need to select the cell below the row(s) and to the right of the column(s) that you want to freeze. After you do that, follow these steps:

1. Click the View menu option.
2. In the Window section, click Freeze Panes.
3. Select Freeze Panes from the drop-down menu in Figure 1.37.

The line above the selected cell and the line to the left of the selected cell are darker. This means that all rows above the darker line and all columns to the left of the darker line are frozen.

Unfreeze Rows and Columns

If you decide that you no longer want a row and/or column frozen, here is how to unfreeze all rows and columns:

1. Click the View menu option.
2. In the Window section in the View ribbon, click Freeze Panes.
3. Select Unfreeze Panes from the drop-down menu.

You only see the Unfreeze Panes option if you have one or more frozen rows and/or columns.

 There are two issues that you will encounter when freezing panes:

- You cannot unfreeze panes by clicking Undo. You must unfreeze panes using the Unfreeze Panes option in the View ribbon.
- You cannot view frozen panes in Page Layout View. If you try to switch to Page Layout View, a dialog box warns you that all cells will be unfrozen. Click OK to unfreeze all panes and view your work in Page Layout view.

Changing Window Views

By default, Excel shows the worksheet in what it calls Normal view, which shows the worksheet. When you need to view the worksheet before you print it to your printer or to a PDF file, you can view where the page breaks are on each page in the Page Break Preview view, as well as how the worksheet will appear on each page in the Page Layout view.

Page Break Preview

View all the page breaks in your worksheet by first clicking the View menu option. Then, in the View ribbon, click the Page Break Preview icon in the Workbook Views section. The worksheet appears with page breaks, as shown in Figure 1.38.

Pages are bordered by a solid blue line. Page breaks are denoted by a dashed blue line. As you scroll up and down the pages, you see gray page numbers in the background, but Excel does not print these page numbers.

Page Layout View

If you need to see how a worksheet appears on printed pages, as well as add a header and/or footer, you need to view your worksheet in Page Layout view.

FIGURE 1.38   Page Break Preview view

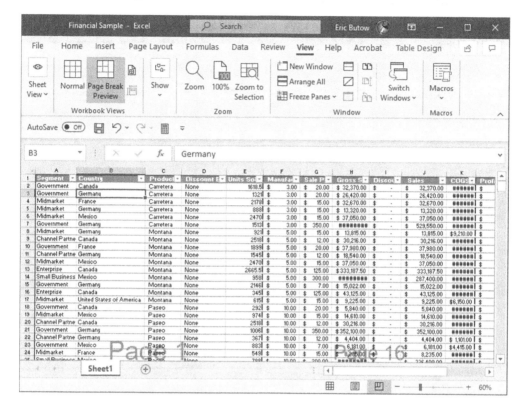

Start by clicking the View menu option. In the View ribbon, click the Page Layout View icon. You see the worksheet contained within graphic representations of pages along with a ruler above and to the left of each page (see Figure 1.39).

Click Add Header at the top of the page and click Add Footer at the bottom of the page to add a header and footer, respectively.

Normal View

If you're viewing the worksheet in Page Break Preview view or Page Layout view, you can return to Normal view by first clicking the View menu option. Then, in the View ribbon, click the Normal icon in the Workbook Views section.

If you're in Page Break Preview view or in Page Layout view and then go back to Normal view, Excel displays page breaks in your worksheet as dashed gray lines. If you want to turn off these page breaks, you must close the worksheet and then reopen it.

FIGURE 1.39 Page Layout view

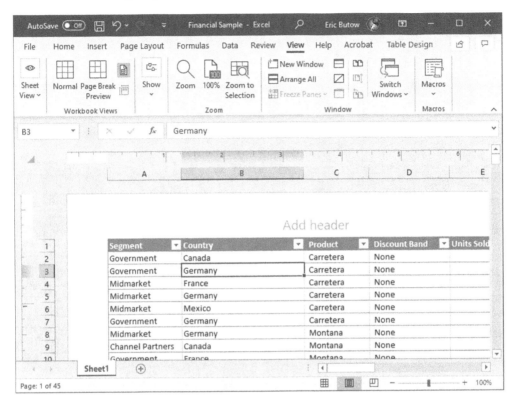

Modifying Basic Workbook Properties

Excel constantly keeps track of basic properties about your workbook, including the size of the workbook file, who last edited it, and when the workbook was last saved.

If you need to see these properties and add some of your own, click the File menu option. In the menu on the left side of the File screen, click Info. Now you see the Info screen, which is shown in Figure 1.40.

The Properties section appears at the right side of the screen. Scroll up and down in the Info screen to view more properties. Excel doesn't show all properties by default, but you can reveal the hidden properties by clicking the Show All Properties link at the bottom of the Properties section.

You can also add properties, including a workbook title, a tag (which is Microsoft's term for a keyword), and a category. For example, click Add A Title in the Properties section to type the workbook title in the box.

FIGURE 1.40   Info screen

Displaying Formulas

Excel gives you ways to display and hide *formulas*, as well as their results, from within a workbook. You can also protect the worksheet to keep your views from being changed by anyone with whom you share your workbook.

Switch Between Displaying Formulas and Their Results

By default, Excel shows the results of a formula within the worksheet but only shows the formula in the Formula Bar above the worksheet.

You can display the formula by pressing Ctrl+`. The grave (`) accent is on the key with the tilde (~) on most keyboards. You can hide the formula again by pressing Ctrl+`.

When you show the formula in the worksheet, the width of the column changes to accommodate as much of the formula as possible. When you show the result again, Excel returns the column width to where it was before you displayed the formula.

Hide a Formula in the Formula Bar

You can hide a formula in the Formula Bar, but only if the worksheet is protected. After you click the cell or select a range of cells with formulas you want to hide, follow these steps:

1. Click the Home menu option, if necessary.

2. In the Cells section in the Home ribbon, click Format. (If the Excel window width is small, click the Cells icon in the ribbon and then select Format from the drop-down menu.)

3. Select Format Cells from the drop-down menu.

4. In the Format Cells drop-down menu, select Protect Sheet, as shown in Figure 1.41.

FIGURE 1.41   Protect Sheet option

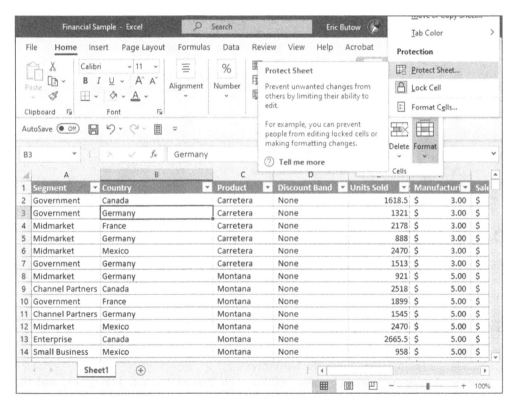

5. Click the Hidden check box.

6. Click OK.

7. Click the Review menu option.

8. In the Protect section in the Review ribbon, click Protect Sheet (see Figure 1.42). (If the Excel window width is small, click the Protect icon in the ribbon and then select Protect Sheet from the drop-down menu.)

FIGURE 1.42   Protect Sheet dialog box

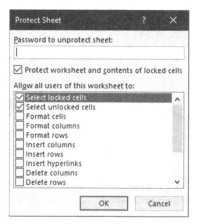

9. In the Protect Sheet dialog box, leave all the check boxes selected. You can add a password in the Password To Unprotect Sheet text box if you plan to share the workbook with anyone else. Otherwise, click OK.

The formula no longer appears in the Formula Bar.

When you hide a formula in the Formula Bar, there is no way to edit the formula until you unprotect the worksheet. You can unprotect the sheet by clicking the Review menu option and then clicking Unprotect Sheet in the Protect section in the Review ribbon.

EXERCISE 1.4

Changing Workbook Properties and Views

1. Open a new or existing workbook.

2. Move the Quick Access Toolbar under the ribbon.

3. Create a custom view of 50 percent magnification.

4. Freeze the first column and row in the worksheet, or the first worksheet in the workbook.

5. View how the worksheet page breaks will appear.

6. Add a title to the workbook.

7. Click a cell in a worksheet that has a formula.

8. Hide the formula in the Formula Bar.

Configuring Content for Collaboration

Excel makes it easy to share workbooks with other people, such as people in the finance, sales, and marketing departments who need to see financial forecasts for the next quarter. Before you do that, you must determine what information you want to share.

You can set a print area within a worksheet, save your workbook in a different format, configure your print settings before you print a document to share on paper or electronically, and inspect your workbook so that you can hide information that you want to keep hidden.

Setting a Print Area

If you print a specific area of rows and columns often, such as a summary of the company's profit and loss for the current quarter, Excel allows you to define a print area within a worksheet.

After you select the cells that you want in the print area within the worksheet, set the print area as follows:

1. Click the Page Layout menu option.

2. In the Page Setup section in the Page Layout ribbon, click Print Area.

3. Click Set Print Area, as shown in Figure 1.43.

4. Click outside the selected area in the worksheet to view the print area, which has a dark gray border around the cell or group of cells in the print area.

Excel saves the print area after you save the workbook.

FIGURE 1.43   Set Print Area option

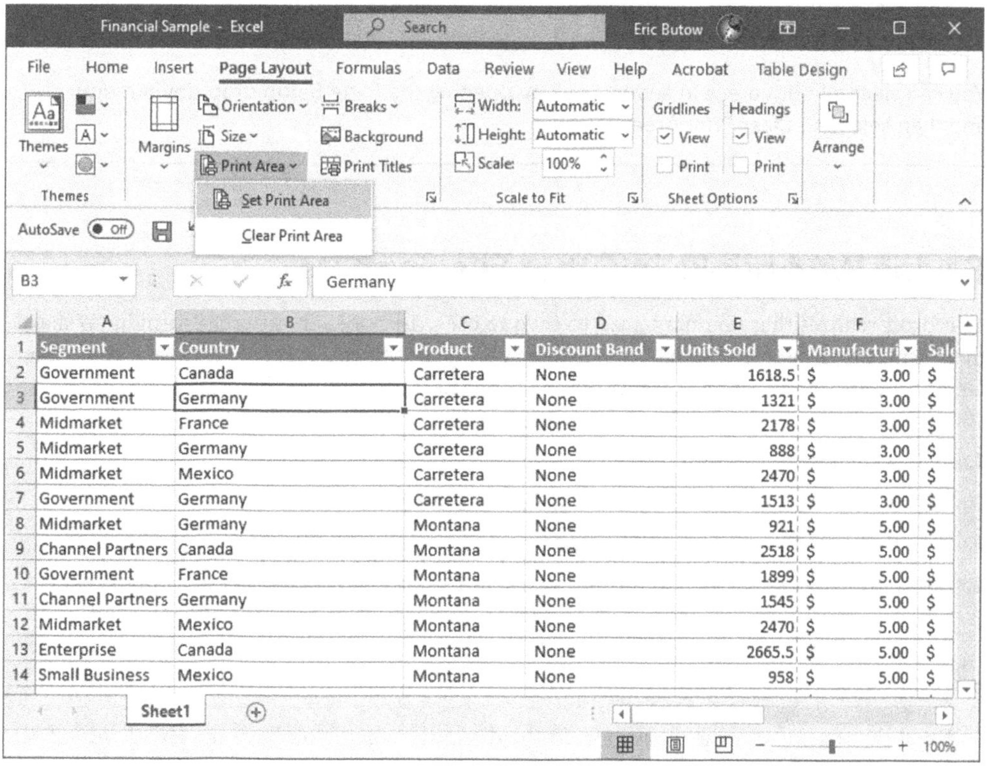

Configuring Print Areas

If you set a single cell as a print area, a dialog box opens and asks you to confirm that this is what you want. Click OK to proceed.

After you set a print area, you can add cells to a print area by selecting one or more cells outside the print area. After you open the View menu ribbon, click Print Area, and then select Add To Print Area from the drop-down menu. The added print area appears with a darker gray line around the cell(s).

You can also set multiple print areas. Each print area prints as a separate page. After you select the first cell or group of cells, hold down the Ctrl key and then select each subsequent cell or group of cells in the worksheet. When you're done, set the print area. Each print area prints as a separate page.

How do you view all of the page areas? Click the View menu option. In the Workbook Views section in the View ribbon, click Page Break Preview. You see all of the print areas in different sections on the screen.

You can clear all print areas in a workbook by opening the Page Setup drop-down menu and then selecting Clear Print Area.

Saving Workbooks in Other File Formats

Microsoft realizes that you may need to save Excel workbooks in different formats to share them with other people who may have older versions of Excel, other spreadsheet apps (like Google Sheets), or no spreadsheet program at all. Rest easy—Excel has you covered.

Here's how to save a workbook in a different file format:

1. Click the File menu option.
2. Click Save As in the menu on the left side of the File screen.
3. On the right side of the Save As screen, click the Excel Workbook (*.xlsx) box.
4. Select one of the file formats from the list shown in Figure 1.44. These formats come from a variety of categories, including older versions of Excel, CSV, HTML, XML, PDF, and text.
5. Click Save.

Excel saves a copy of the worksheet in the directory where you have the Excel worksheet. Your Excel worksheet remains active so that you can continue to work on it if you want.

After you save to some file formats such as delimited text, you may see a yellow warning bar above the worksheet warning you that you may have some data loss. This bar also displays buttons that you can click to hide the bar in the future or to save the Excel file in a different format.

Configuring Print Settings

Before you print to either a printed page or to PDF format, you can view the print preview settings and make changes in Excel.

Excel easily detects the default printer that you're using in Windows and lets you change the printer settings so that your document appears on paper the way you want.

Start by clicking the File menu option, and then click Print in the menu on the left side of the File screen. Now you see the Print screen, and the print preview area appears on the right side so that you have a good idea of what the worksheet will look like on the printed page.

FIGURE 1.44   A partial list of file formats

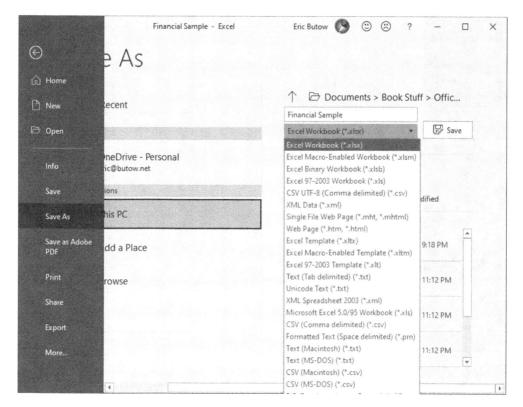

Between the menu area on the left and the print preview area, the Settings menu you see depends on the printer you have.

In my case, I can change the printer to another one that I have installed in Windows, as shown in Figure 1.45. I can also change different settings for the selected printer, including how many pages to print, the page orientation, and whether I should print on one or both sides of the paper.

Inspecting Workbooks for Issues

Before you share a workbook with other people, such as in an email attachment, you should take advantage of the Document Inspector in Excel to find information that you may not realize is saved with your workbook. For example, Excel saves author information, and you may not want to share that information when you share the workbook with someone outside your company.

FIGURE 1.45   Print screen

 Before you inspect your workbook and perhaps remove some information, you may want to save a copy of your workbook and remove the information from that copy. Excel may not be able to restore data when you click Undo in the Quick Access Toolbar, or press Ctrl+Z, so it's better to be safe than sorry.

Start by clicking the File menu option. Click Info in the menu bar on the left side of the File screen. Now that you're in the Info screen, click the Check For Issues button. From the drop-down list, select Inspect Document.

Now you see the Document Inspector dialog box, as shown in Figure 1.46. Scroll up and down the list of content that Windows will inspect.

By default, the following check boxes next to the content category names are selected:

- Comments
- Document Properties And Personal Information
- Data Model
- Content Add-Ins

FIGURE 1.46   Document Inspector dialog box

- Task Pane Add-Ins
- PivotTables, PivotCharts, Cube Formulas, Slicers, and Timelines
- Embedded Documents
- Macros, Forms, And ActiveX Controls
- Links To Other Files
- Real Time Data Functions
- Excel Surveys
- Defined Scenarios
- Active Filters
- Custom Worksheet Properties
- Hidden Names
- Ink
- Long External References
- Custom XML Data
- Headers And Footers

- Hidden Rows And Columns
- Hidden Worksheets
- Invisible Content (which is content that has been formatted as such but that does not include objects covered by other objects)

These check boxes mean that the Document Inspector will check content in all those areas. Select Ink, the only clear check box, if you want to check whether someone has written in the workbook with a stylus, such as the Microsoft Surface Pen.

When you decide what you want Excel to check out, click Inspect. When Excel finishes its inspection, you can review all the results in the dialog box.

The results show all content categories that look good by displaying a green check mark to the left of the category name. If Excel finds something that you should check out, you see a red exclamation point to the left of the category. Under the category name, Excel lists everything it found. Remove the offenders from your workbook by clicking the Remove All button to the right of the category name.

You can reinspect the workbook by clicking Reinspect as often as you want, until you see that all of the categories are okay. When you're done, click the Close button to return to the Info screen.

When you remove hidden rows, columns, or even worksheets that contain data, you may find that calculations and formulas no longer give you the results you want. . .or fail entirely. If you are not sure what will happen if you remove hidden data in a workbook, unhide the affected cells and inspect them before Excel does.

EXERCISE 1.5

Changing Print Settings and Inspecting a Workbook

1. Open a new workbook, and then add text in two columns and five rows.

2. Save the workbook.

3. Select all cells in the first three rows.

4. Set a print area in the selected cells.

5. Select all cells in the fourth row and then add those cells to the print area.

6. Save a copy of the workbook as a CSV file.

7. Inspect the worksheet and remove all problems found.

Summary

This chapter started by showing you how to import data stored in TXT and CSV files into Excel. Aside from Excel-formatted files, you will most likely receive other files from text and CSV-formatted files because those formats are ubiquitous.

Next, I discussed how to navigate within a workbook. You can search for data; navigate to named cells, ranges, and other workbook elements; and insert and remove hyperlinked text within a cell.

Then, you learned how to format worksheets and workbooks to look the way that you want. You learned how to modify the page setup, adjust row width and column height, and customize headers and footers.

You then went further by learning how to customize Excel and its options so that features in the Excel window look the way you want. Those customization features include customizing the Quick Access Toolbar, displaying and modifying the look of workbook content, freezing worksheet rows and columns, changing window views, modifying basic workbook properties, and displaying formulas.

Finally, you learned how to configure your content for collaboration. You learned how to set a print area in a worksheet and workbook, save a workbook in a different file format, configure your print settings, and inspect workbooks for issues, including hidden content that you don't want to share.

Key Terms

AutoFit	hyperlinks
comma-delimited value	range
delimiter	wildcard
footer	workbook
formulas	worksheet
header	

Exam Essentials

Understand how to import TXT and CSV files into a worksheet.   Know how to import files in both TXT and CSV formats into a worksheet using the built-in file import tools.

Know how to search for data in a workbook.   Understand how to search for data by using the Find And Replace feature in Excel to find search terms in a worksheet or all the sheets in a workbook, and then replace your search term(s) with other terms and/or formatting.

Understand how to navigate to different elements in a workbook.   Know how to go to different elements using the Go To feature to go to a specific cell, range of cells, or another worksheet in your workbook.

Know how to insert and remove hyperlinks.   Understand how to insert a hyperlink within a cell and remove a hyperlink if you want.

Understand how to format worksheets and workbooks.   Know how to use Excel formatting tools to format worksheets and workbooks, including how to modify the page setup, adjust row height and column width in a worksheet, and customize headers and footers.

Be able to set and change Excel options and spreadsheet views.   Know how to change options and views, including how to customize the Quick Access Toolbar, display content in different views, modify workbook content in different views, change window views, freeze worksheet rows and columns, modify basic workbook properties, as well as display and hide formulas.

Know how to set a print area and configure print settings.   Understand how to set a print area within a worksheet and configure your print settings, including changing the printer, the worksheet(s) to print, and the page orientation.

Understand how to save workbooks in other file formats.   Know the file formats to which Excel can save a workbook, how to select the format you want, and how to save the workbook in your preferred format.

Be able to inspect workbooks for issues.   Know how to inspect a workbook before you share it, including how to look for hidden information contained in the Excel file that you may not want to share, how to check for accessibility issues, and how to check for compatibility issues.

Review Questions

1. What kinds of characters can be a delimiter? (Choose all that apply.)
   - **A.** Tab
   - **B.** Semicolon
   - **C.** Comma
   - **D.** Period

2. How do you search for a cell that has the question mark in the text?
   - **A.** Search for the question mark character.
   - **B.** Type a tilde before the question mark.
   - **C.** Add two question mark characters in a row.
   - **D.** Type the grave accent mark before the question mark.

3. How do you make a column fit to the text that takes up the most width in a cell within that column?
   - **A.** Use the mouse to drag the right edge of the column until it's the size of the text.
   - **B.** Double-click at the right edge of the cell.
   - **C.** Double-click at the right edge of the column in the header.
   - **D.** Triple-click at the right edge of the column in the header.

4. What can you add to the Quick Access Toolbar? (Choose all that apply.)
   - **A.** Styles
   - **B.** Tools
   - **C.** Views
   - **D.** Commands

5. What formats can Excel save to? (Choose all that apply.)
   - **A.** PDF
   - **B.** Text
   - **C.** Word
   - **D.** Web page

6. Where can you place the Quick Access Toolbar? (Choose all that apply.)
   - **A.** Under the ribbon
   - **B.** In the ribbon
   - **C.** In the menu bar
   - **D.** In the title bar

7. How do you provide additional information for a link within a cell?

    A. Type the description in the cell after the link.

    B. Add a Screen Tip.

    C. Type the description in a cell adjacent to the link.

    D. Right-click the link to view more information.

8. In what view do you add a header or footer?

    A. Custom Views

    B. Page Break view

    C. Page Layout view

    D. Normal view

9. How do you hide a formula in the Formula Bar?

    A. By right-clicking the Formula Bar and then clicking Hide

    B. By using the Home menu ribbon

    C. By protecting the worksheet

    D. By using the View menu ribbon

10. What menu ribbon do you use to set a print area?

    A. View

    B. Home

    C. Data

    D. Page Layout

Chapter

2

Using Data Cells and Ranges

MICROSOFT EXAM OBJECTIVES COVERED IN THIS CHAPTER:

✓ **Manage data cells and ranges**

- ▪ Manipulate data in worksheets
    - ▪ Paste data by using special paste options
    - ▪ Fill cells by using Auto Fill
    - ▪ Insert and delete multiple columns or rows
    - ▪ Insert and delete cells
- ▪ Format cells and ranges
    - ▪ Merge and unmerge cells
    - ▪ Modify cell alignment, orientation, and indentation
    - ▪ Format cells by using Format Painter
    - ▪ Wrap text within cells
    - ▪ Apply number formats
    - ▪ Apply cell formats from the Format Cells dialog box
    - ▪ Apply cell styles
    - ▪ Clear cell formatting
- ▪ Define and reference named ranges
    - ▪ Define a named range
    - ▪ Name a table
- ▪ Summarize data visually
    - ▪ Insert Sparklines
    - ▪ Apply built-in conditional formatting
    - ▪ Remove conditional formatting

After you add data into a worksheet, you probably need to make changes to make the text and numbers work the way you want. Manipulating data can be repetitive—not to mention boring—but you have Excel tools at your disposal to make your job faster and easier.

Those tools include a wide variety of paste options, Auto Fill (to add sequential data like numbers and dates), the ability to insert and delete multiple rows and columns, as well as the ability to insert and delete cells.

Once you have the data the way you want it, you may want to format cells the way you want. Excel gives you the tools that you need to merge (and unmerge) cells, modify how data appears in a cell, use Format Painter (which you may know from Word), wrap text in a cell, apply cell and number formats, and apply cell styles. If you need to remove a style from text, Excel has you covered there, too.

A nice time-saving feature when you're searching for data or want to add data in a group of cells to a formula is the ability to name a range of cells. You can also name a table, and this chapter offers a sneak peek at using tables (you will learn more in Chapter 3, "Working with Tables and Table Data").

Finally, you will learn how to summarize data visually using the Sparklines feature to add visual data about a specific group of cells. You'll also learn how to apply conditional formatting, such as when you need to highlight a group of cells to make an important point to your readers.

Manipulating Data in Worksheets

Microsoft knows that copying and pasting data, inserting data, and filling in data is a core component of all its Microsoft 365 programs. Without this functionality, Microsoft 365 would not exist, let alone be the standard suite of office applications for businesses.

Excel, like its sibling programs in Microsoft 365, has copying and pasting data down cold. You can also use other tools, such as Auto Fill to speed up data entry, as well as tools that help with inserting and deleting cells, rows, and columns more quickly.

Pasting Data by Using Special Paste Options

In Chapter 1, "Managing Worksheets and Workbooks," you learned about some basic data paste options. Excel contains a slew of paste options so that the pasted text looks the way you want.

After you open a workbook, or you have created a new one and entered some data, select a cell to copy by clicking the cell. Click the Home menu option (if necessary), and then click Copy in the Clipboard section in the ribbon—or you can press Ctrl+C.

Next, click the cell where you want to paste the data. Now view your paste options by clicking the down arrow under the Paste icon in the Clipboard section. The drop-down menu is divided into three sections, as shown in Figure 2.1.

FIGURE 2.1   The Paste drop-down menu

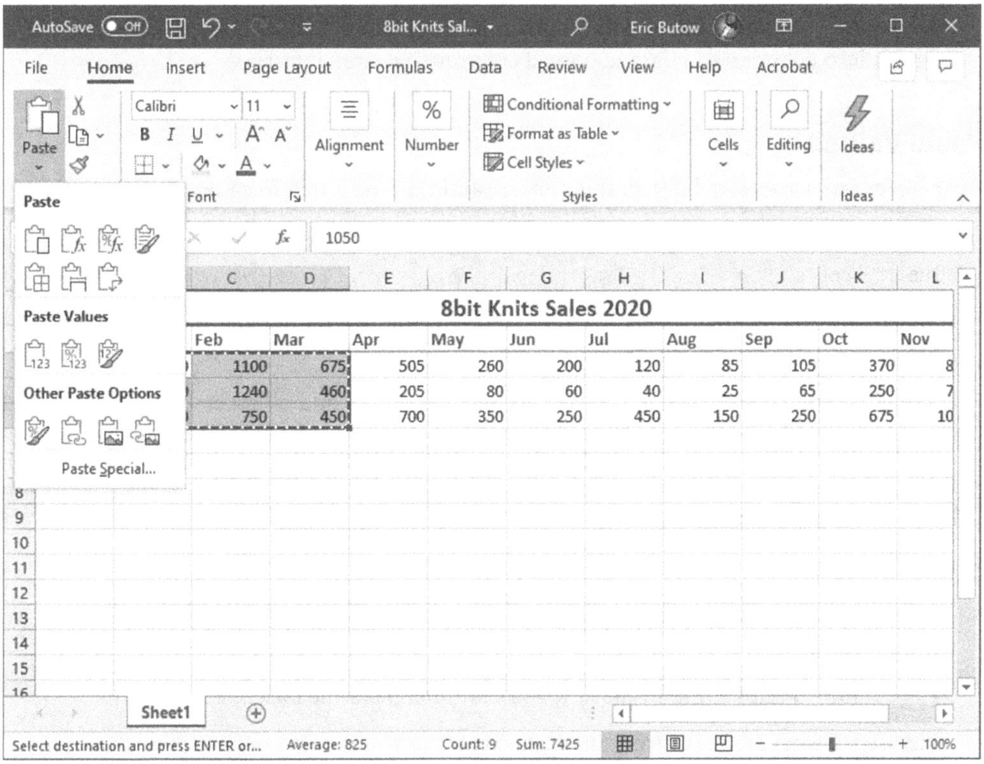

Paste

The seven icons in this section are listed from left to right, top to bottom:

Paste   Pastes all data in the copied cell, including formulas and formatting, into the new cell

Formulas   Pastes the formulas without any formatting from the copied cell into the new cell

Formulas & Number Formatting   Pastes only the formulas and number formatting from the copied cell into the new cell

Keep Source Formatting   Pastes all text formatting from the copied cell into the new cell

No Borders   If the copied cell has a cell border, then Excel does not paste the cell border into the new cell.

Keep Source Column Widths   Excel resizes the column width in the new cell to match the width of the copied cell.

Transpose   Changes the orientation of copied cells so that data in copied rows is pasted into columns and data in copied columns is pasted into rows

Paste Values

Only three options are available in this section, and they are listed from left to right:

Values   Pastes all formula results without any formatting from the copied cell into the new cell

Values & Number Formatting   Pastes formula results with number formatting from the copied cell into the new cell

Values & Source Formatting   Pastes all formula results and all formatting in the copied cell to the new cell

Other Paste Options

This section contains four icons, which are listed from left to right:

Formatting   Pastes only the formatting, but none of the data, from the copied cell(s) to the new cell(s)

Paste Link   Pastes a link in the new cell that references the copied cell

Picture   Pastes an image from the copied cell(s) into the new cell(s)

Linked Picture   Pastes an image from the copied cell(s) along with a link to the original cell(s) into the new cell(s). When you make changes to the image in the original cell(s), Excel updates the new cell(s) with the new image automatically.

Paste Special

If you don't see the paste option you want, the Paste Special link appears at the bottom of the drop-down menu, as you saw in Figure 2.1. After you click the link, the Paste Special dialog box appears (see Figure 2.2).

FIGURE 2.2   Paste Special dialog box

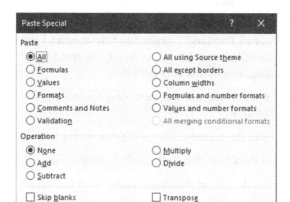

Click one of the following options in the dialog box. Note that you can only click one option in the Paste section and only one option in the Operation section. You can also click one or both check boxes below the Operation section.

All   Pastes all contents and formatting from the copied cell(s) into the new cell(s)

Formulas   Pastes only the formulas from the copied cell(s) into the new cell(s)

Values   Pastes only the values, not the formulas, of the copied cell(s) into the new cell(s)

Formats   Pastes only the formatting in the copied cell(s) into the new cell(s)

Comments And Notes   Pastes only comments and notes with the copied cell(s) into the new cell(s)

Validation   Pastes data validation rules in the copied cell(s) into the new cell(s). *Validation* controls what users can enter in a cell, such as five numbers for a ZIP code.

All Using Source Theme   Pastes all cell contents that have document theme formatting from copied cell(s) into new cell(s)

All Except Borders   Pastes all cell contents and formatting, but not cell borders, from copied cell(s) into new cell(s)

Column Widths   Excel resizes the column width in the new cell(s) to match the width of the copied cell(s)

Formulas And Number Formats   Pastes only formulas and number formatting from the copied cell(s) into the new cell(s)

Values And Number Formats   Pastes only values and number formatting from the copied cell(s) into the new cell(s)

All Merging Conditional Formats   Pastes all of the data and conditional formatting options in the copied cell(s) into the new cell(s). If the copied cell(s) does not have any conditional formatting, this option is grayed out.

None   Excel will not perform any mathematical operations when it pastes copied data into one or more new cells.

Add   Adds data from the copied cell(s) to the data in the new cell(s)

Subtract   Subtracts data from the copied cell(s) from the data in the new cell(s)

Multiply   Multiplies data from the copied cell(s) with the data in the new cell(s)

Divide   Divides data from the copied cell(s) by the data in the new cell(s)

Skip Blanks   When you copy one or more blank cells, Excel will not put a value in the corresponding new cell(s)

Transpose   Changes the orientation of copied cells so that data in copied rows is pasted into columns and data in copied columns is pasted into rows

If you click Paste Link, the dialog box closes, and you create a link to the copied cell(s) within the new cell(s). If you don't want to add a link, click OK. The pasted cell(s) reflect the options you selected in the dialog box.

Filling Cells by Using Auto Filling

As you enter data in a worksheet, you may find yourself wondering why you have to keep entering the same data over and over, or why you have to type in a sequence of numbers or even dates. The Excel Auto Fill feature makes it easy to fill cells with the same data or a data sequence.

Start by adding data into a cell. You can add the following types of data:

- The same number or a series of numbers, such as 10, 20, and so forth
- The abbreviated or full day of the week, such as Mon or Monday
- The abbreviated or full month of the year, such as Jan or January
- The date in mm/dd format, such as 10/15

If you're repeating only one number in other cells, type the number in the first cell. If you're adding a series of numbers, type the first two numbers into the first two cells in a row or column.

If you want to add a series of the same number or letter, or if your data is a month name (like January) or date (like 10/15), type the first number, month name, or date into the first cell in the row or column.

Next, move the mouse pointer to the green dot in the lower-right corner of the selected cell. The pointer changes to a plus sign. Click and hold the left mouse button, and then drag over the cells that you want to fill. As you drag, a small pop-up box appears above the pointer that tells you what value will be filled in the cell (see Figure 2.3).

FIGURE 2.3   Pop-up box shows what value you will fill.

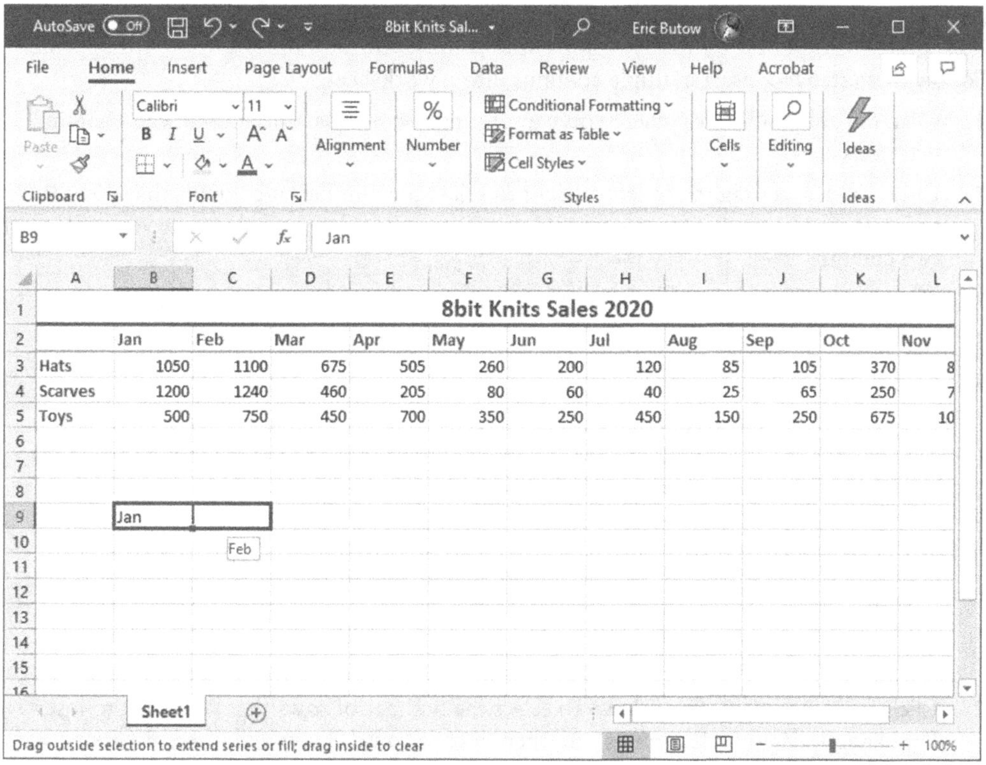

	A	B	C	D	E	F	G	H	I	J	K	L
1					8bit Knits Sales 2020							
2		Jan	Feb	Mar	Apr	May	Jun	Jul	Aug	Sep	Oct	Nov
3	Hats	1050	1100	675	505	260	200	120	85	105	370	8
4	Scarves	1200	1240	460	205	80	60	40	25	65	250	7
5	Toys	500	750	450	700	350	250	450	150	250	675	10
6												
7												
8												
9		Jan										
10			Feb									
11												
12												
13												
14												
15												

Cell reference box: B9, formula bar: Jan

Status bar: Drag outside selection to extend series or fill; drag inside to clear

When you drag over all the cells that you want to fill, release the mouse button. Excel fills the cells with the months, dates, or number sequence.

 NOTE   If you fill more rows than there are 7 days in a week or 12 months in a year, then Excel starts over after the day or month sequence finishes. For example, Excel starts over again on Monday in the seventh empty column or row that you fill.

Inserting and Deleting Multiple Columns or Rows

As you work with data, you may need to insert multiple columns or rows, such as when you need to add a new expense with a particular month. You may also need to delete a row or column, such as when you don't want to include a column to identify a type of product. Excel allows you to insert multiple columns and rows at once to save you time and effort.

Insert Multiple Columns

Follow these steps to insert multiple columns into a worksheet:

1. Click the column header where you want to insert columns. The column can contain text in its cells.
2. Click, hold, and drag to the left or right to select the number of columns that you want to insert. For example, if you select column C and then drag to column D, you will insert two columns.
3. When you select the number of columns to insert, release the mouse button.
4. Right-click one of the selected columns.
5. Click Insert in the pop-up menu.

The number of inserted columns with blank cells is highlighted in the worksheet. If you selected columns that had populated cells, those columns move to the column immediately to the right of the inserted columns (see Figure 2.4).

Insert Multiple Rows

Here's how to insert multiple rows into a worksheet:

1. Click the row header where you want to insert rows. The row can contain text in its cells.
2. Click, hold, and drag up or down to select the number of rows that you want to insert. For example, if you select row 5 and then drag to row 10, you will insert six rows.
3. When you select the number of rows to insert, release the mouse button.
4. Right-click one of the selected rows.
5. Select Insert from the pop-up menu.

The number of inserted rows is highlighted in the worksheet. If you selected rows that had populated cells, those rows move to the row immediately below the inserted rows (see Figure 2.5).

FIGURE 2.4 Inserted columns

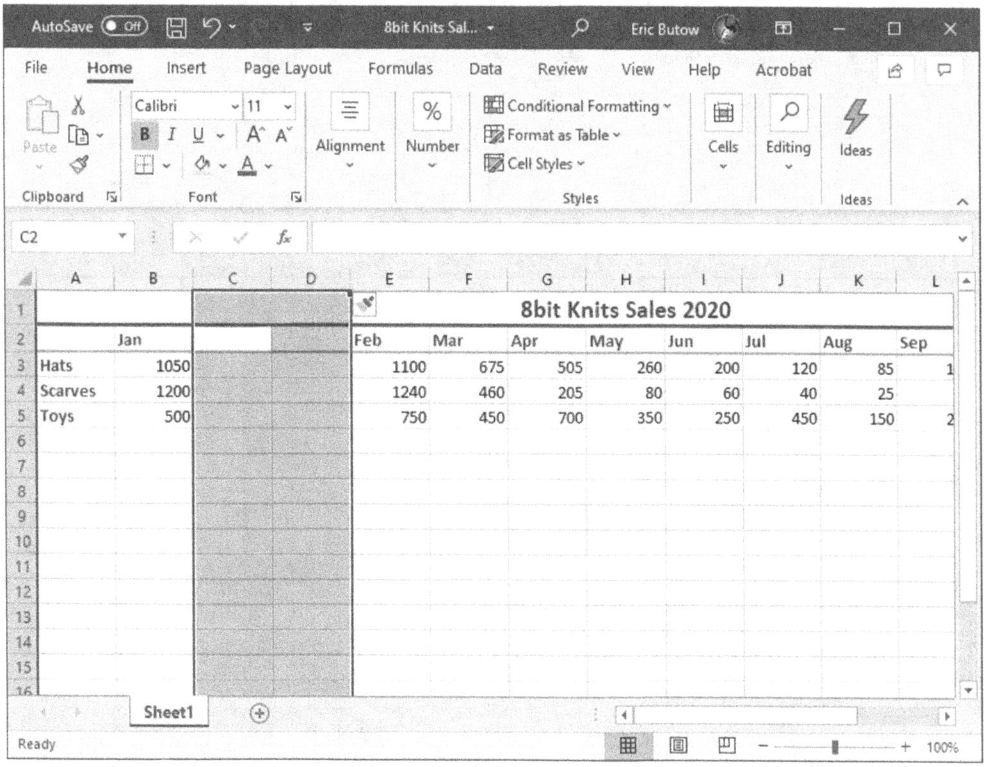

Deleting Multiple Rows and Columns

You can delete rows and columns much as you did when you inserted them. Here's how:

1. Click the row or column header where you want to delete rows or columns.
2. Click, hold, and drag left and right for columns, or up and down for rows, to select the number of columns or rows that you want to insert. For example, if you select row 5 and then drag to row 10, you will delete six rows.
3. After you have selected the rows or columns, release the mouse button.
4. Right-click one of the selected rows.
5. Select Delete from the pop-up menu.

The selected cells disappear. Any columns to the right of the deleted columns move left, and any rows below the selected rows move up.

FIGURE 2.5   Inserted rows

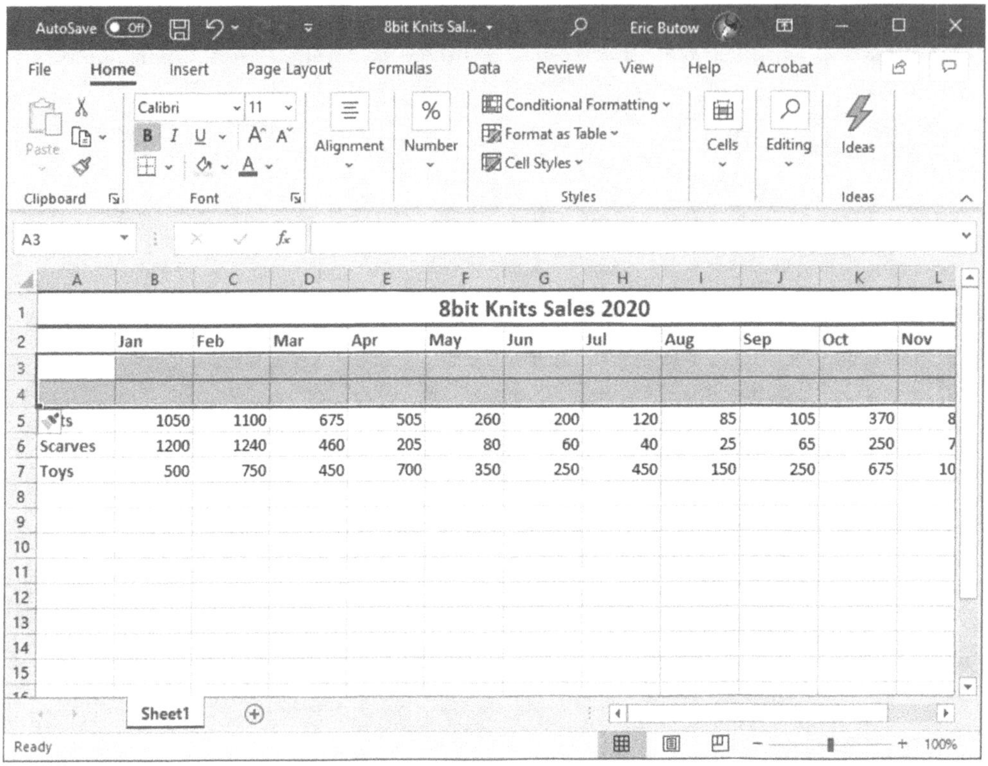

Adding and Removing Cells

Adding and removing cells is a part of life when you edit a worksheet. Deleting data in a cell is as easy as clicking the cell and then pressing Delete on your keyboard. You can delete data in all cells within a row or column by clicking the row or column header and then pressing Delete.

You can also delete a column or row as well as all of the data within it by following the instructions in one of the following two sections.

Add and Remove a Column

Insert a column by clicking the column header above the column. In the Home ribbon, click the Insert icon in the Cells section. (If your Excel window width is small, click the Cells icon and then click the Insert icon.) Then select the Insert Sheet Columns option from the drop-down menu, as shown in Figure 2.6.

FIGURE 2.6   Insert Sheet Columns menu option

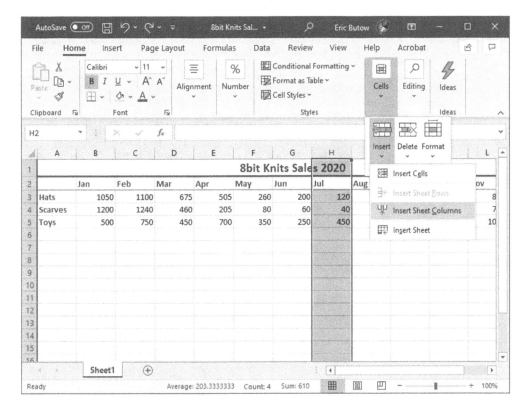

All columns to the right of the selected column move one column to the right.

You can delete a selected column by clicking the Delete icon in the Cells section in the ribbon, and then selecting the Delete Sheet Columns option from the drop-down menu. All columns to the right of the deleted column move to the left.

Insert and Delete a Row

Insert a row by clicking the row header to the left of the row. In the Home ribbon, click the Insert icon in the Cells section. (If your Excel window width is small, click the Cells icon and then click the Insert icon.) Then select the Insert Sheet Rows option from the drop-down menu, as shown in Figure 2.7.

All rows below the selected row move one row down.

You can delete a selected row by clicking the Delete icon in the Cells section in the ribbon and then selecting the Delete Sheet Rows option from the drop-down menu. All rows below the deleted row move up.

FIGURE 2.7   Insert Sheet Rows menu option

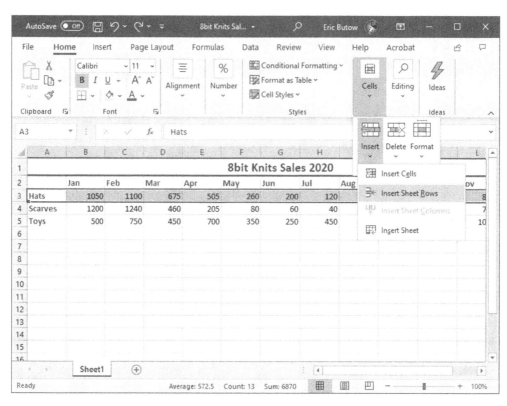

 When you select a row or column that has formatting, such as bold text, applied to it, Excel applies that formatting to the new row or column that you insert.

EXERCISE 2.1

Manipulating Data

1. Open an existing workbook or create a new workbook and add data in four columns and four rows.

2. Copy one cell and paste it to a blank cell.

3. Insert a new column.

4. Auto Fill all 12 months of the calendar.

5. Insert two rows within the third row of the worksheet.

6. Delete the second column from the worksheet.

Formatting Cells and Ranges

Another common editing task is formatting cells or a group of cells, which Excel calls a *range*. Excel includes tools for merging and unmerging cells and modifying cells to look the way you want. Use Format Painter to format text in cells quickly, just as with text in Word; wrap text around images in your worksheet; format numbered lists; and apply styles to cells—a task that, you guessed it, is similar to Word's.

Merging and Unmerging Cells

It's easy to merge multiple cells into one. A common example is making a title row. You type the title into row 1, column 1 in the worksheet. Then you select several contiguous cells within the same row and click Merge & Center in the Home ribbon. The title appears centered across all the columns that you selected.

Start by clicking the cells you want to merge in a row, and then click the Home menu option (if necessary). In the Alignment section in the Home ribbon, click the down arrow to the right of Merge & Center. (If your Excel window width is small, click the Alignment icon and then click the down arrow to the right of Merge & Center.)

Now you can select from one of three merge options in the drop-down menu, as shown in Figure 2.8:

Merge & Center   Merges all the selected cells in the merge area and centers the text contained in the upper-left cell within the merged area. If you merge multiple rows, Excel vertically aligns the text at the bottom of the merged cells.

Merge Across   Merges all the selected cells in the row(s) but keeps the text in the upper-left cell aligned left. If you merge cells in multiple rows, Excel merges each row separately.

Merge Cells   Merges all selected cells in the merge area and keeps the text in the upper-left cell aligned left within the merged area.

When you need to unmerge cells, click the merged cell and then click the down arrow to the right of Merge & Center in the Home ribbon. Then select Unmerge Cells from the drop-down menu, as you saw in Figure 2.8.

What You Can and Can't Do When Merging

If you try to merge cells when more than one cell in the merge area has text in them, a dialog box appears that reminds you that only text in the upper-left cell within the merge area is intact in the merged cell. When you click OK, you see the text from the upper-left cell in the merged cell. Excel deletes all the text in the other cells.

You also cannot split an unmerged cell into smaller cells. If you need smaller cells, reduce the width of the column in which the cell resides.

FIGURE 2.8   Merge options in the drop-down menu

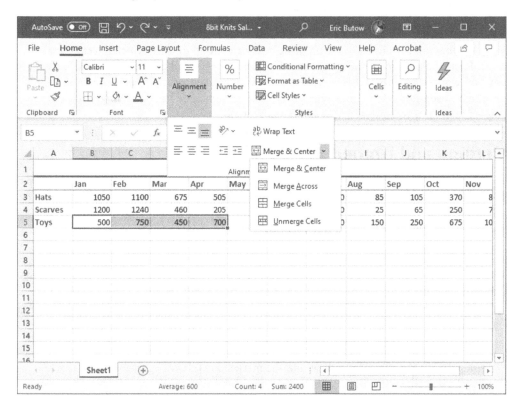

Modifying Cell Alignment, Orientation, and Indentation

When you have the data in a worksheet the way you want, you can change how the cell looks when other people read it. Excel gives you the power to change the cell alignment and orientation, and to align the cell differently so that it stands out from the rest of the text and/ or numbers.

Align a Column or Row

When you need to align data in rows or columns to appear a certain way, such as numbers in a column right-aligned in every cell, here's how to do that:

1. Select the cell(s), column(s), and/or row(s) that you want to align. You can align data in a single cell if you want.

2. Click the Home menu option, if necessary.

3. In the Alignment section in the Home ribbon, click the Align Left, Center, or Align Right icon, as shown in Figure 2.9. (If your Excel window width is small, click the Alignment icon and then click the down arrow to the right of Merge & Center.)

FIGURE 2.9   Align Left, Align Center, and Align Right icons

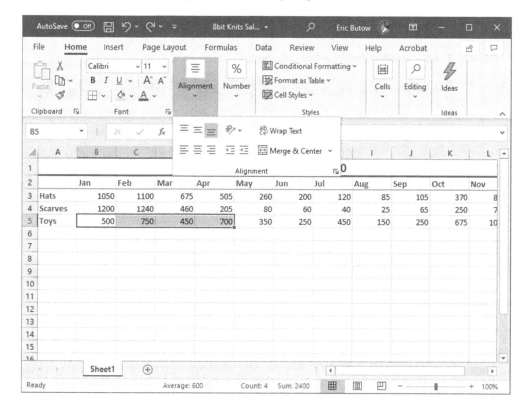

The default alignment for cells is Align Left. If you want to align the cells vertically, click the Top Align, Middle Align, or Bottom Align icon. The default vertical alignment in all cells is Bottom Align.

 If you want to select all cells in a worksheet quickly, click a blank cell and then press Ctrl+A.

Change the Orientation of Text in a Cell

You may want to change the orientation of data in a cell, a range of cells, a row, or a column by changing the text rotation. For example, you may want to rotate text in the first row 90 degrees. Change the orientation by following these steps:

1. Select the cell, range, row(s), or column(s).

2. Click the Home menu option, if necessary.

3. In the Alignment section in the Home ribbon, click the Orientation icon. (If your Excel window width is small, click the Alignment icon and then click the Orientation icon.)

4. Select one of the options in the menu shown in Figure 2.10.

FIGURE 2.10   Orientation drop-down menu

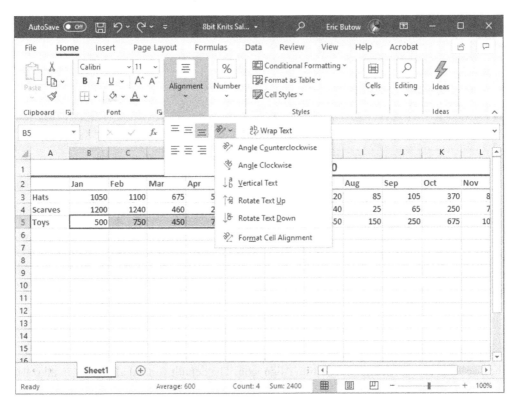

You can select from one of the following options:

Angle Counterclockwise: Rotates the text 45 degrees

Angle Clockwise: Rotates the text –45 degrees

Vertical Text: Makes the text vertical but does not rotate the text so that each letter appears on a separate line of text

Rotate Text Up: Rotates the text 90 degrees (counterclockwise)

Rotate Text Down: Rotates the text –90 degrees (clockwise)

Rotate Text to a Precise Angle

If you need to rotate text to a specific angle instead of the built-in angles that Excel provides, open the Orientation drop-down menu and then click Format Cell Alignment.

In the Format Cells dialog box (see Figure 2.11), the Alignment tab is selected by default.

FIGURE 2.11   Format Cells dialog box

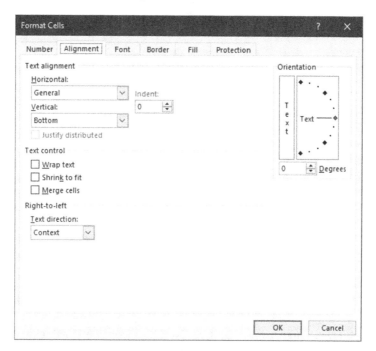

On the right side of the dialog box, type the number of degrees in the Degrees box in either positive or negative numbers. The preview area above the box shows you how the text will look. You can also increase or decrease the degrees by one degree by clicking the up and down arrows, respectively, to the right of the Degrees box.

You will learn more about the Format Cells dialog box later in this chapter.

Formatting Cells by Using Format Painter

All Microsoft 365 programs include the Format Painter feature, which is a quick and easy way to apply formatting from selected data in a cell to data in another cell. Follow this process to get started:

1. Select the text or click text in a paragraph that has the formatting you want to copy.

2. Click the Home menu option if it's not selected already.

3. In the Home ribbon, click the Format Painter icon in the Clipboard section, as shown in Figure 2.12.

FIGURE 2.12 Format Painter icon

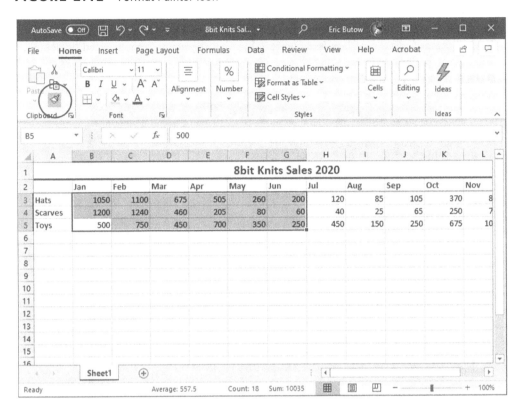

The mouse pointer changes to the standard Excel plus icon combined with a paintbrush. Now you can select text in another cell. The text in the cell that you selected now shows the format you copied.

> **NOTE**
> This process works only once, but you can change the format of multiple blocks of text. After you select the text with the formatting that you want to copy, double-click the Format Painter icon in the Home toolbar and then select the cells. When you're done, press the Esc key.

Wrapping Text Within Cells

After you change the width of a column, the text within the selected column stays on the screen. If you want the text to stay within the column width, you can wrap the text. You can also add line breaks within text so that you have better control of where the text wraps in a cell.

Wrap Text

When you want to wrap text, start by selecting the cell(s), range, row(s), or column(s). Next, click the Home menu option, if necessary. In the Home menu ribbon, click Wrap Text in the Alignment section, as shown in Figure 2.13. (If your Excel window width is small, click the Alignment icon and then click Wrap Text.)

FIGURE 2.13 Wrap Text option

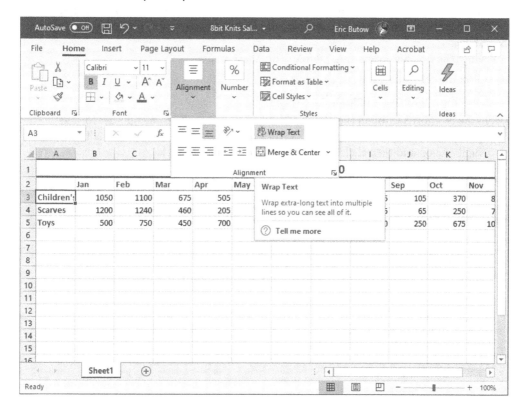

Excel automatically wraps the text within the width of the column(s). Change how the wrapped text appears in the cell(s) by changing the width of each affected column.

Add a Line Break

When you need a line break within text in a cell, start by double-clicking the cell. The text cursor appears within the text. Now click on the location within the text where you want to add the line break, and then press Alt+Enter.

The text after the line break appears on a new line and may appear in front of text in the cell underneath the cell you're editing. Click outside the cell to view the text with your line break. Excel automatically increases the height of the cell and the entire row to accommodate the text on multiple lines.

Wrapping text and line breaks do not work with numbers or formulas in a cell. When you reduce the width of a column so that a number cannot fit within the cell width, Excel places pound or hash (#) marks in the cell instead.

Using Number Formatting

You may need to change the format of your numbers for easier reading. For example, if your numbers denote currency, you may want to add the appropriate currency symbol in front of the number.

Change the number formatting by following these steps:

1. Select the cell, range, row(s), or column(s).
2. Click the Home menu option, if necessary.
3. In the Number section in the Home ribbon, click one of the three number format options that are shown in Figure 2.14. (If your Excel window width is small, click the Number icon and then click one of the number format icons.)

FIGURE 2.14 Number format options

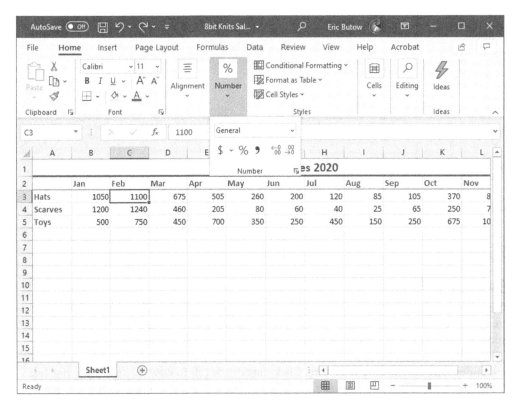

You can click the Accounting Number Format icon (which is a $ symbol), the Percent Style icon (%) to add a percentage with the number, or the Comma Style icon (which looks like a large comma) to apply a comma within a number larger than 999. If you apply a number format to an empty cell, then you won't see the formatting until you type a number into it.

If you need to view all number formats, click the down arrow next to the General button in the Number section. You can view more number formats in the Format Cells dialog box, which has the Number tab open by default. You will learn more about the Format Cells dialog box in the next section.

Applying Cell Formatting from the Format Cells Dialog Box

The Format Cells dialog box contains all the format styles that you can apply to data within cells. Open the dialog box by clicking the Home menu option (if necessary), and then clicking Format in the Cells section. (If your Excel window width is small, click the Cells icon and then click Format.)

Now select the Format Cells option at the bottom of the drop-down menu, which is shown in Figure 2.15.

The Format Cells dialog box appears (see Figure 2.16) with the Number tab active by default.

You can select from one of the following tabs to view all formatting options and change them as you see fit:

Number   Allows you to set 11 different specific number formats to one or more cells, from Number to a custom format. The default selection is General, which means that there is no specific number format.

Alignment   Allows you to change the text alignment, control, direction, and/or orientation in one or more cells

Font   Shows the current font and font style assigned to the cell. The default is 11-point Calibri. You can change the font, the font style, and the font size; apply effects; and apply a color.

Border   Allows you to add a border on one or more sides of a cell or a range

Fill   Displays the current background of the cell or range. The default is No Color, but you can select a fill color, set a pattern, and add a fill effect.

Protection   Allows you to lock and/or hide a cell or a range in the worksheet

FIGURE 2.15   Format Cells option

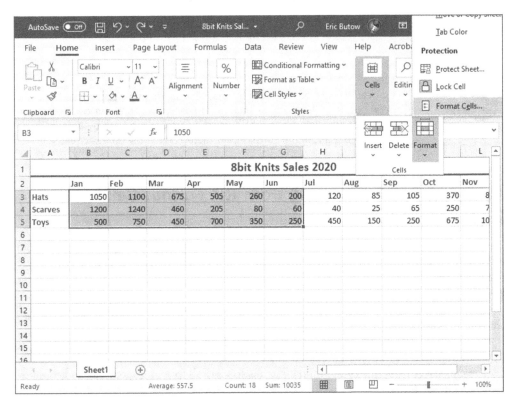

Working with Cell Styles

You can apply styles to a cell within the Home menu ribbon without having to open the Format Cells dialog box. You can also apply prebuilt styles or add your own. A *style* is a set of format settings that you can apply so that you don't have to apply each format setting one at a time.

Apply a Cell Style

Start by selecting the cell or the range of cells, and then click the Home menu option, if necessary. In the Styles section in the Home menu ribbon, click the Cell Styles icon in the Styles section. The Cell Styles drop-down list appears below the icon (see Figure 2.17).

FIGURE 2.16   Format Cells dialog box

A selected style has a white border around the style tile, and the default style is Normal. You can apply a prebuilt style by clicking one of the style tiles in one of the following list sections:

- Good, Bad, and Neutral
- Data and Model
- Titles and Headings
- Themed Cell Styles
- Number Format

After you apply the style, Excel applies the style formats to the cell(s). If you apply a style to a blank cell, the cell may show some of the style formatting, such as a color in the cell background.

FIGURE 2.17   Cell Styles drop-down list

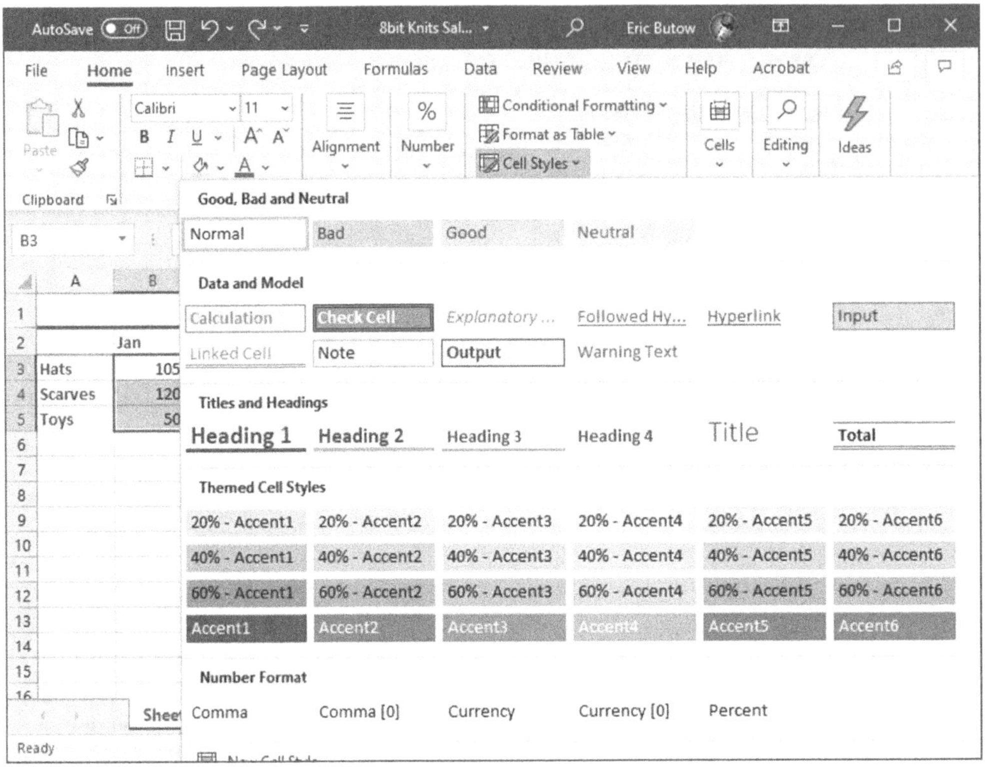

Remove a Cell Style from Data

If you decide that you don't want a style applied to a cell or range anymore and want to revert to the default format, select the cell or range. Next, open the Cell Styles drop-down list as you did in the previous section, and click Normal in the Good, Bad, and Neutral section.

Clearing Cell Formatting

If you need to clear formatting from a cell, Excel gives you several options. For example, you may have text in a cell as a hyperlink and you want to remove the hyperlink but keep the rest of the cell formatting intact.

Here's how to clear one or more formats from a cell or range of cells:

1. Select the cell, range, row(s), or column(s).

2. Click the Home menu option, if necessary.

3. In the Editing section in the Home ribbon, click Clear. (If your Excel window width is small, click the Editing icon and then click Clear.)

Now you can select from one of the six options in the Clear drop-down list, shown in Figure 2.18:

Clear All: Clears all contents, including formats and comments from the cell(s)

Clear Formats: Clears all formats from the cell(s) but leaves the contents and leaves intact any comments and/or notes attached to the cell(s)

Clear Contents: Clears all contents in the cell(s) but leaves the formatting and any attached comments and/or notes intact

Clear Comments and Notes: Clears all comments and/or notes attached to the cell(s) but leaves contents and formatting intact

Clear Hyperlinks: Clears all hyperlinks from the cell(s) but keeps the formatting. That is, the text in the cell(s) is still blue and underlined but has no functioning link

Remove Hyperlinks: Clears all hyperlinks and formatting from the cell(s)

FIGURE 2.18   Clear drop-down list

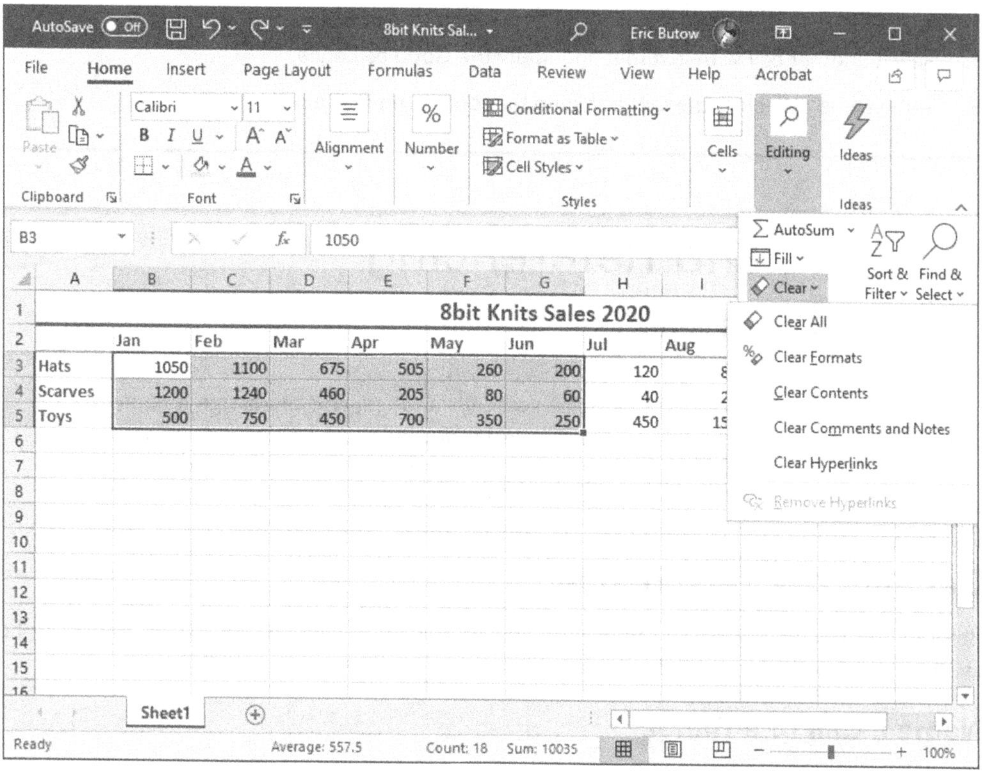

If you click Clear All or Clear Contents, the cell no longer contains a value. Any formula that refers to that cleared cell returns a value of 0.

EXERCISE 2.2

Formatting Cells and Ranges

1. Open an existing workbook.

2. Create a new row at the top of the worksheet.

3. Select all the cells in the new row that span the width of the rest of the worksheet and then merge and center those cells.

4. Add new text in an empty cell and then rotate the text up.

5. Copy one style in a cell to another cell with Format Painter.

6. Select a cell and then add a separate line of text within that cell.

7. Select another cell and then change the cell color to blue.

8. Select another cell with text in it and apply the Good cell style.

9. In the same cell, clear the text but keep the formatting in the cell.

Defining and Referencing Named Ranges

When you select a group of cells, which Excel calls a *range*, you can assign a name to each range that you select. This feature makes it easier not only to find a range you want in a worksheet or workbook, but also to add a link to a named range within a formula in another cell.

Defining a Named Range

Before you can add a link to a range, you need to select and name a range. That range can be as small as one cell. After you name the range, you can add it to a formula.

Name a Cell or a Range

Here's how to attach a name to a cell or a range:

1. Select the cell or range in the worksheet.

2. Click the Formulas menu option.

3. In the Defined Name section in the Formulas ribbon, click Define Name. (If your Excel window width is small, click the Defined Names icon.)

4. Select Define Name from the drop-down list, as shown in Figure 2.19.

FIGURE 2.19   Define Name option

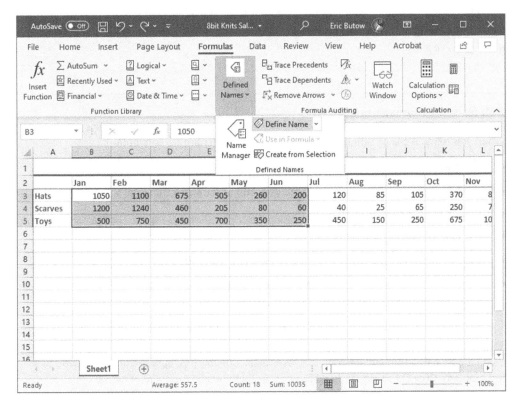

5. In the New Name dialog box, shown in Figure 2.20, type the name of the cell by pressing Backspace and then typing the new name in the Name text box. This name can be up to 255 characters long.

FIGURE 2.20   New Name dialog box

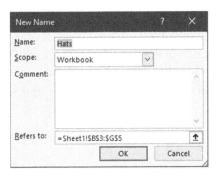

6. Click Workbook to select the scope of the range. Workbook is the default option, which means that any formula in the workbook can refer to the named cell. If you select the worksheet in the drop-down list, Excel applies the name only to the selected cells in that worksheet.

7. Add a comment up to 255 characters long in the Comment text box.

8. The Refers To box in the New Name dialog box reflects the cell location where you're adding the name, so leave this box as is.

9. Click OK.

Cell Naming Conventions

When you name a cell or range, you need to follow Excel naming conventions:

- The name must start with a letter or an underscore (_).

- You can use only letters, numbers, periods, and underscore characters.

- Names are not case sensitive.

- You cannot include spaces within a name.

- You can use the same name format as a cell reference, such as A1.

- Do not use the single letters C and R to name a range because Excel uses these letters for shortcuts to select a column and row, respectively.

- You cannot use an existing name in the workbook, even if the name you want to use is capitalized and the other one is not.

If you type a name that violates one of these rules, a dialog box appears that alerts you to the problem. Click OK to close the dialog box so that you can type a new name.

Define Names from a Selected Range

If you prefer to use a name based on text in one or more of the selected cells, you can create a name from the selection by following these steps:

1. Select the range in the worksheet.

2. Click the Formulas menu option.

3. In the Defined Name section in the Formulas ribbon, click Define Name. (If your Excel window width is small, click the Defined Names icon.)

4. Select Create From Selection from the drop-down list shown in Figure 2.21.

FIGURE 2.21   Create From Selection option

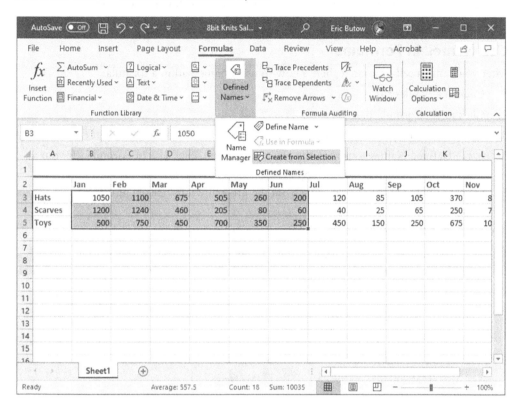

5. In the Create Names From Selection dialog box, shown in Figure 2.22, select one or more of the four Create Names From Values In check boxes: Top Row, Left Column, Bottom Row, or Right Column. (Excel may have one or more of these selected based on your selection.)

FIGURE 2.22   Create Names From Selection dialog box

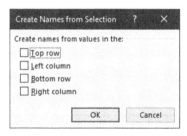

6. Click OK.

You may see a series of dialog boxes asking you to confirm that you want to change the names of different cells in the range. Click OK in each dialog box to complete the renaming process.

Use Names in Formulas

After you name a cell or a range, here's how to use a name within a formula:

1. Click in a blank cell.
2. Click in the Formula Bar.
3. Click the Formulas menu option.
4. In the Defined Names section in the Formulas ribbon, click Use In Formula. (If your Excel window width is small, click the Defined Names icon.)
5. Select the name of the cell or range from the drop-down list (see Figure 2.23).

FIGURE 2.23 Use In Formula drop-down menu

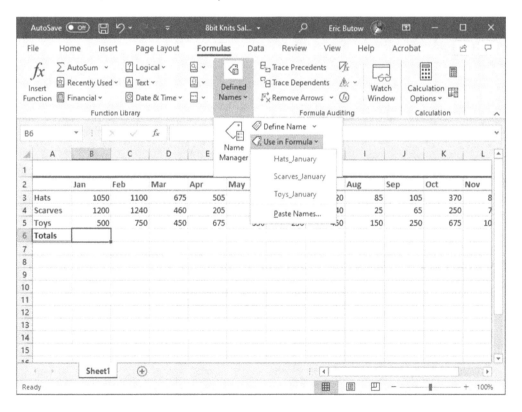

The cell name appears in the Formula Bar, and then you can continue to build the formula as you see fit.

Naming a Table

As in Word, you can add a separate table in an Excel worksheet. (You will learn more about creating tables in Chapter 3.) You can name a table in a worksheet, just as you can name a cell so that you can refer to it next time.

Start by clicking the table in the worksheet. Now follow these steps:

1. Click the Table Design menu option.

2. In the Properties section in the Table Design ribbon, click the table name in the Table Name Box, as shown in Figure 2.24. The default name is Table1, but you may see a different name.

FIGURE 2.24   Highlighted table name in the Table Name Box

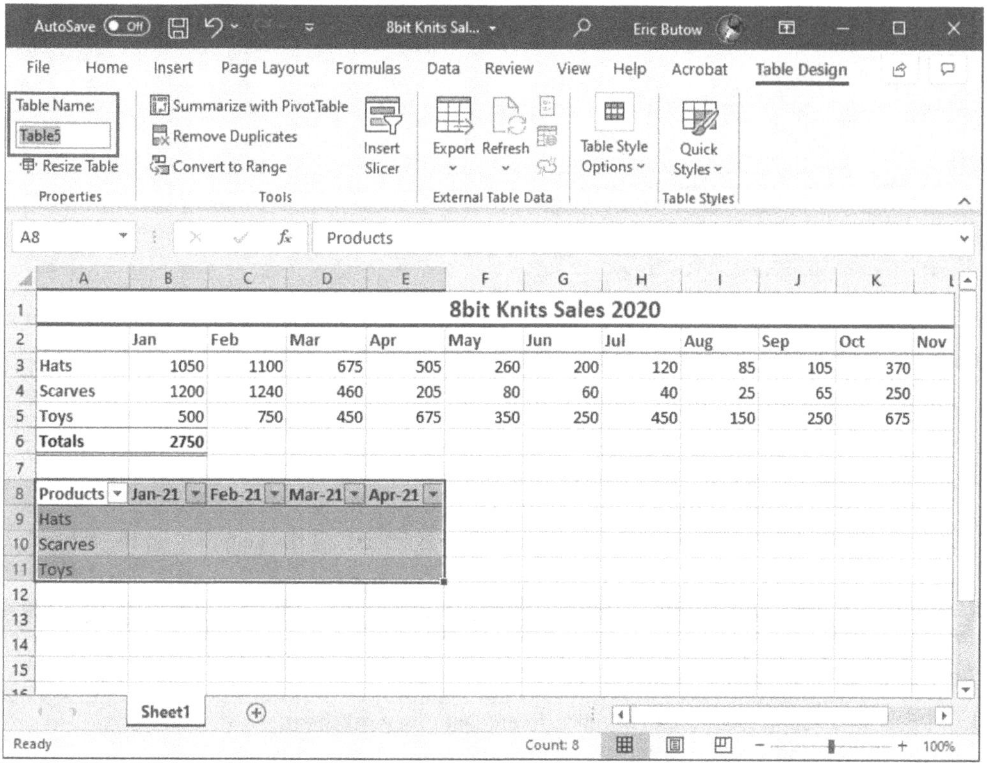

3. Press Backspace and then type the new name, as shown in Figure 2.24.

4. Press Enter.

When you want to go to the table quickly, click the down arrow in the Name Box, which is to the left of the Formula Bar. Then click the table name, as shown in Figure 2.25.

FIGURE 2.25   Highlighted table in the Name Box

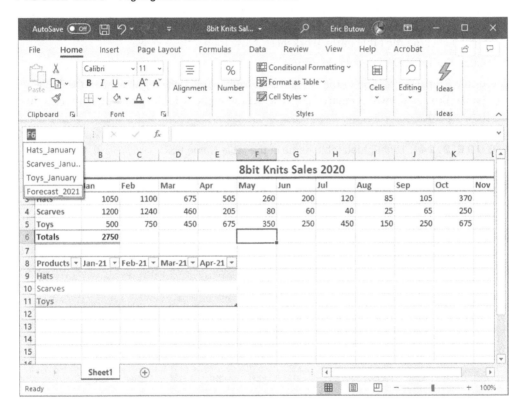

Excel moves to the table within the worksheet and selects all the cells within the table.

EXERCISE 2.3

Define and Reference Named Ranges

1. Open an existing workbook with data in at least one worksheet.

2. Create one bulleted list with four items.

3. Select a range of cells and name the range.

4. Select a second range of cells, and then name the range from cells in the top row.

5. Click an empty cell.

6. Add a formula that adds the two named ranges and view the result.

Summarizing Data Visually

Graphical charting has been an integral part of all spreadsheet programs since Lotus 1-2-3 introduced charting in 1983. Excel has taken visual representation of data down to small pieces of data that you can chart to show trends using *Sparklines*.

You can also point out data in a worksheet by using conditional formatting for some cells. As the name implies, you change the conditions of cells to show different visual cues in each cell.

Inserting Sparklines

A *Sparkline* is a tiny chart that appears in a cell and does not include any text data. So, a Sparkline is a great way to give a quick glance of a trend, such as product sales over a specific period. You can add three types of Sparkline charts: Line, Column, and Win/Loss.

After you add a Sparkline, you can format it to look the way you want. For example, you can change the color of a line chart to appear green to tell your audience that sales are growing.

Add a Sparkline

You add a Sparkline at the end of a row of data. For example, if you have monthly sales totals in row 6, and the last column of data is in column F, then place your cursor in cell G6.

Now add the Sparkline by following these steps:

1. Click the Insert menu option.

2. In the Sparklines section in the Insert ribbon, click the Line, Column, or Win/Loss icon, as shown in Figure 2.26. (If your Excel window width is small, click the Sparklines icon and then click one of the three icons.)

3. In the Create Sparklines dialog box, shown in Figure 2.27, type the data range of the cell, such as E1:E6, or select all the cells in the worksheet that you want to add to the data range. After you select all the cells, Excel populates the data range in the Data Range text box.

4. Click OK.

FIGURE 2.26   The three Sparkline icons

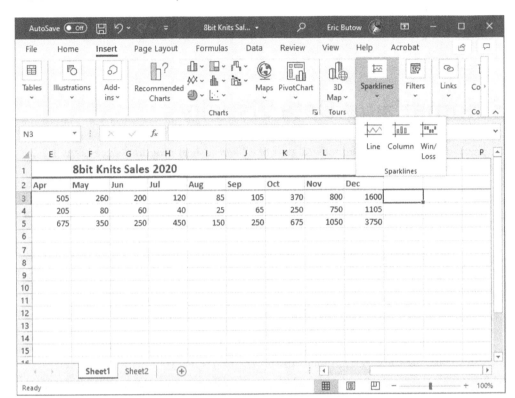

FIGURE 2.27   The selected cell range

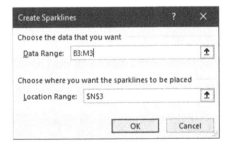

The small Sparkline chart appears in the cell to give readers a visual representation of the numbers in the row. For example, if you add a Line Sparkline chart, you see a line that curves up and down to reflect the ups and downs of numbers in each column within the row.

If you want to enlarge the Sparkline chart, increase the size of the row and the column that contains the chart.

Format a Sparkline Chart

After you add a Sparkline chart, the cell with the chart is highlighted and the Sparkline menu ribbon opens automatically (see Figure 2.28) so that you can format your chart the way you want.

FIGURE 2.28   Sparkline menu ribbon

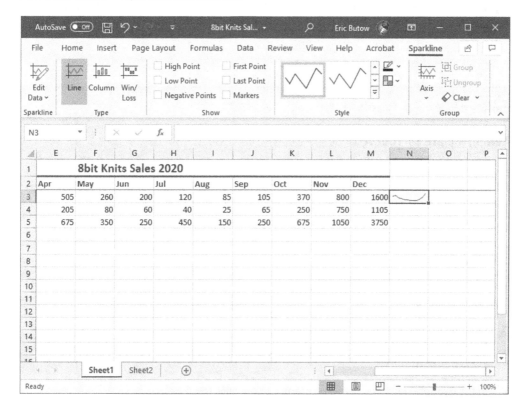

Now you can select functions in the following sections in the ribbon:

Sparkline   Click the Edit Data text below the Edit Data icon so that you can edit a group or single cell of data in a Sparkline chart, and change how empty or hidden cell settings appear in a Sparkline chart.

Type   Change the Sparkline chart type by clicking the Line, Column, or Win/Loss icon.

Show   Allows you to show different points within the Sparkline chart, such as where the high and low points are located.

Style   Change the colors of the Sparkline chart to one in a prebuilt style that you can choose, or change the colors to ones that you prefer.

Group   Show and change the horizontal and vertical axis settings, group and ungroup Sparkline charts, and clear a Sparkline chart from the cell.

You can't delete a Sparkline chart by clicking the cell and then pressing Delete. You must clear the Sparkline chart from the cell in the Group section in the ribbon.

 Real World Scenario

Adding a Date to Your Axis

Your boss has told you that she likes your Sparklines because they give her a quick, at-a-glance data trend within a row. However, she noticed something troubling: in the cells, sales numbers for every month aren't available and she wants to know why.

After you explain that you haven't received any information for those months from the sales team, she wants to see that reflected in the Sparkline chart in part to remind her about the missing months.

But how do you change the Sparkline chart to show missing months within the chart? Follow these steps:

1. Click the Sparkline chart in the worksheet.

2. Change the chart type to Column. (This solution won't work if you select one of the other two types.)

3. In the Group area in the Sparkline menu ribbon, click the Axis icon.

4. Select Date Axis Type from the drop-down menu.

5. Select the cells that contain dates within the worksheet. For example, you may have the dates in the first row of the worksheet. The selected cells appear in the Sparkline Date Range dialog box.

6. Click OK in the dialog box.

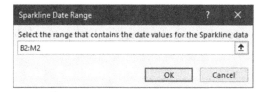

The Sparkline column chart shows bars in some columns and no bars in others. The areas with no bars show no data for those dates and gives a good visual representation to your boss about why she should call out the sales team for not giving you the data you need.

Applying Built-In Conditional Formatting

Excel lets you highlight cells in a range that you want readers to pay attention to. For example, when you get sales numbers from the sales department and plug those numbers into your spreadsheet, your conditional formatting for the sales totals for the month can change color depending on how much was made and how it compares to the target amount.

Start by selecting a range of cells. The *Quick Analysis* icon appears next to the lower-right corner of the selected range (see Figure 2.29).

FIGURE 2.29 Quick Analysis icon

	A	B	C	D	E	F	G	H	I	J	K	L
1					8bit Knits Sales 2020							
2		Jan	Feb	Mar	Apr	May	Jun	Jul	Aug	Sep	Oct	Nov
3	Hats	1050	1100	675	505	260	200	120	85	105	370	
4	Scarves	1200	1240	460	205	80	60	40	25	65	250	
5	Toys	500	750	450	675	350	250	450	150	250	675	
6	Totals	2750										

When you move the mouse pointer over the button, a pop-up box explains what the icon is about. Click the icon to open the drop-down menu that appears below the icon, as shown in Figure 2.30.

After you select a cell or range, you can press Ctrl+Q to open the Quick Analysis drop-down menu.

FIGURE 2.30   Quick Analysis drop-down menu

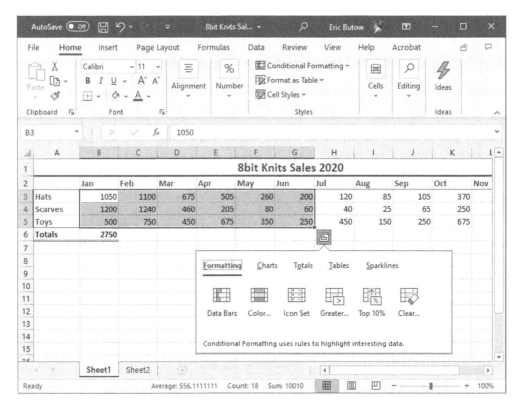

The Formatting tab is open by default, so you can select a formatting type by clicking the icon in the menu. When you move the mouse pointer over an icon, you see a preview of how the data will look in your selected cells once you click the icon.

The icons available in the pop-up box depend on the data you selected in the cells. For example, if you select cells with text, then you will see different formatting options than you would have if you had selected cells that contained only numbers, or cells with both numbers and text.

The example in Figure 2.30 has a range of numbers selected. Click on one of the following six format type icons:

Data Bars: Shows transparent data bars within each cell to show the amount in each cell compared to the largest value in the range

Color: Adds colors to cells in a manner that Excel thinks is relevant. For example, low numbers in the range will have red-colored cells and high numbers will have green-colored cells.

Icon Set: Adds up (green), down (red), and right (yellow) arrow icons to the left of every number to show relationships between numbers in the range (You may not agree with how Excel assigns an arrow to a cell.)

Greater: Opens the Greater Than dialog box so that you can assign a color to all cells with values that are over a certain number. For example, you can assign green to all cells with a value over 5,000.

Top 10%: Places the color in one or more cells that are within the top 10 percent of all values in the range

Clear: Clears all formatting from the range

When you click one of the icons, the drop-down menu disappears. You can open the Quick Analysis pop-up box again to view the drop-down menu and select an additional format style. For example, if you click Color and then click Icon Set, you will see the colors and the icons in all cells in the range.

If you don't see the preview in your cell or range when you move the mouse pointer over it, this means that you cannot use that format option in your cells.

For example, if you select cells with text, and there is no duplicate text in two or more cells within the range, then when you move the mouse pointer over the Duplicate icon, nothing happens because there is no duplicate text to show.

Removing Conditional Formatting

You can remove conditional formatting from an entire worksheet and within a selected range of cells. If you remove conditional formatting within a worksheet, you can clear all formats or all instances of only one format.

Clear Conditional Formatting on a Worksheet

Here's how to clear all conditional formatting throughout an entire worksheet:

1. Click the Home menu option if it's not selected already.

2. In the Styles section in the Home menu ribbon, click Conditional Formatting.

3. Move the mouse pointer over Clear Rules in the drop-down menu.

4. Click Clear Rules From Entire Sheet, as shown in Figure 2.31.

FIGURE 2.31   Clear Rules From Entire Sheet option

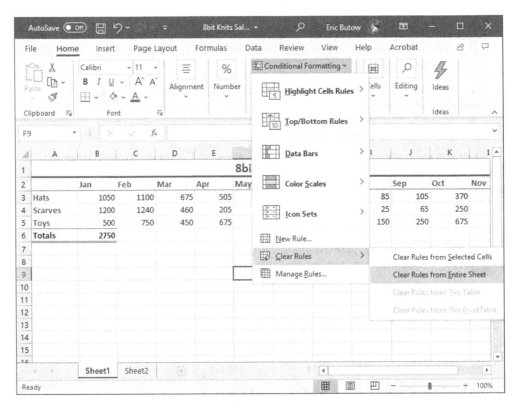

In a Range of Cells

If you want to remove conditional formatting only from a range of cells, follow these steps:

1. Select the range in the worksheet.

2. Click the Home menu option if it's not selected already.

3. In the Styles section in the Home menu ribbon, click Conditional Formatting.

4. Move the mouse pointer over Clear Rules in the drop-down menu.

5. Click Clear Rules From Selected Cells, as shown in Figure 2.32.

FIGURE 2.32   Clear Rules From Selected Cells option

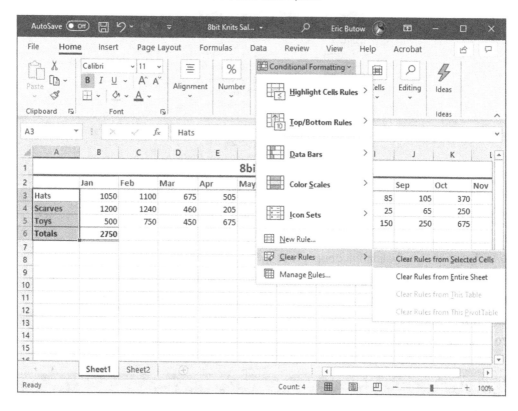

 You can also open the Quick Analysis drop-down menu and click the Clear icon, as you learned earlier in this chapter.

Find and Remove the Same Conditional Formats Throughout a Worksheet

If you need to find all cells that have the same conditional formats throughout the worksheet, there is no easy way to do that. However, you can use the Find And Replace feature in Excel to find all instances of conditional formats in a row and then delete them. Here's how:

1. Click the cell that contains the conditional format that you want to remove.
2. Click the Home menu option if it's not selected already.
3. In the Editing section in the Home ribbon, click Find & Select. (If your Excel window width is small, click the Editing icon and then click Find & Select.)
4. Select Go To Special from the drop-down menu.
5. In the Go To Special dialog box, shown in Figure 2.33, click the Conditional Formats option.

FIGURE 2.33   Go To Special dialog box

6. Under the Data Validation option, click the Same button.

7. Click OK. Excel highlights all cells that have the conditional formatting in the row.

8. In the Styles section in the Home menu ribbon, click Conditional Formatting.

9. Move the mouse pointer over Clear Rules in the drop-down menu.

10. Click Clear Rules From Selected Cells, as you saw in Figure 2.32.

EXERCISE 2.4

Summarizing Data Visually

1. Open a new worksheet.

2. Add the months of the year within row 1.

3. Type numbers into all 12 columns within row 2 and row 3.

4. Add a Sparkline line chart in row 2.

5. Add a Sparkline column chart in row 3.

6. Apply color formatting to all the cells in row 2 and row 3.

7. Apply a data bar to all the cells in row 3.

8. Remove formatting within the first six columns in row 2.

Summary

This chapter started by showing you how to paste data using a variety of special paste options in Excel. Next, you learned how to fill in cells automatically using the Auto Fill feature. You also learned how to insert and delete multiple columns, rows, and cells.

After you saw how to add data into a worksheet, you learned how to format cells and a range of cells. I discussed how to merge and unmerge cells. Next, you learned how to modify cell alignment, orientation, and indentation. I showed you how to format cells using Format Painter and discussed how to wrap text within cells. Then you saw how to apply number formats, cell formats, and cell styles. And you learned how to clear one or more formats from one or more cells.

Next, I discussed how to define a named range, reference the named range in a formula, and name a table so that you can find it easily. Finally, you learned how to insert Sparkline charts, apply built-in conditional formatting to one or more cells, and remove conditional formatting.

Key Terms

Auto Fill	Sparklines
Format Painter	transpose
Quick Analysis	validation
range	wrap text

Exam Essentials

Understand how to paste and fill cells.   Know how to access data paste options and which option is right for your situation. You also need to understand how to use the Auto Fill feature to fill in repeating or sequential data in a range of cells.

Know how to insert and delete cells, rows, and columns.   Understand how to add and delete cells as a row and a column, as well as insert and delete multiple rows and columns.

Understand how to format cells and ranges of cells.   Know how to merge and unmerge cells; modify alignment, orientation, and indentation of data within a cell; format cells using Format Painter; wrap text within cells; apply number formats; apply cell formats and styles; and clear cell formatting.

Know how to define a named range.   Understand how to define a range of cells and refer to the named range in a formula.

Understand how to name a table.   Be able to name a table and move your cursor to the named table in a worksheet.

Be able to insert Sparklines.   Know how to add a Sparkline chart and change its format to summarize information in a row quickly.

Know how to apply and remove conditional formatting.   Understand how to add and apply conditional formatting to a range of cells, find cells with conditional formatting, and remove conditional formatting from a cell range.

Review Questions

1. What option do you use to paste formula formatting from one cell into a new cell?

   A. Paste Formulas

   B. Formulas And Number Formatting

   C. Paste

   D. Keep Source Formatting

2. What option do you use when you want to merge text but not affect the alignment?

   A. Merge Cells

   B. The Align Left icon in the Home ribbon

   C. Merge Across

   D. Merge & Center

3. What types of text can you use as the first character when you name a range? (Choose all that apply.)

   A. Numbers

   B. Letters

   C. Only the letters C or R

   D. Underscores

4. How do you select all cells in a worksheet quickly?

   A. Right-click a cell, and then click Select All in the context menu.

   B. Click the Find & Select icon in the Home menu ribbon, and then click Select All in the drop-down menu.

   C. Click the 100% icon in the View menu ribbon.

   D. Press Ctrl+A.

5. Where do you place a Sparkline chart?

   A. After the last column in a row

   B. Below the first column in a row

   C. Above the first column

   D. In the first row and column in a worksheet

6. What type of data can you use with Auto Fill? (Choose all that apply.)

   A. Dates

   B. Numbers

   C. Text

   D. Months of the year

7. What option do you use in the Orientation drop-down menu to give text a specific angle?

    A. Angle Counterclockwise

    B. Angle Clockwise

    C. Format Cell Alignment

    D. Rotate Text Up

8. What Quick Analysis formatting option do you use to show cell colors based on numeric criteria?

    A. Top 10%

    B. Color

    C. Greater

    D. Data Bars

9. How long can a named range be?

    A. 127 characters

    B. An unlimited length

    C. 255 characters

    D. Only as many characters as will fit in the text box

10. What types of currency number formats can you apply? (Choose all that apply.)

    A. Accounting Number style

    B. Fraction style

    C. Percent style

    D. Comma style

Chapter

3

Working with Tables and Table Data

MICROSOFT EXAM OBJECTIVES COVERED IN THIS CHAPTER:

✓ **Manage tables and table data**

- Create and format tables
    - Create Excel tables from cell ranges
    - Apply table styles
    - Convert tables to cell ranges
- Modify tables
    - Add or remove table rows and columns
    - Configure table style options
    - Insert and configure total rows
- Filter and sort table data
    - Filter records
    - Sort data by multiple columns

It may sound strange to talk about tables in an Excel spreadsheet. After all, isn't a worksheet just one giant table? Actually, a table in Excel is a specific object that contains a number of additional features that make your data easier to work with.

I start this chapter by showing you how to create a table and how the functionality in a table differs from data in a worksheet. After you create a style, you will learn how to apply a built-in table style. And if you have a table, you will learn how to convert a table back into a cell range.

Next, I will show you how to modify tables further. Excel allows you to add and remove table rows and columns easily. If you want to add a table style, you will learn how to configure them. And when you want to add total rows to a table, you will see how to insert and configure those.

Finally, you'll learn how to filter and sort data in your tables so that they look the way you want.

Creating and Formatting Tables

A table looks a lot like the cells in a worksheet, but an Excel table has plenty of built-in features that you can create more easily than you can within a worksheet.

These features include a header row, which appears by default at the top of the table. The *header row* in each column contains functionality to sort and filter data within the column. You can also add a formula in one column and apply that formula to other columns in your table.

Excel allows you to create tables from existing cell ranges, and vice versa. The Table Design menu ribbon also lets you format your table with different built-in or custom styles.

Creating Excel Tables from Cell Ranges

If you have existing cells in your worksheet and you decide that you want to put them into a table to take advantage of table functionality, here's how to create an Excel table from a range of cells:

1. Select the cell range.
2. Click the Home menu option, if necessary.
3. In the Styles section in the Home ribbon, click Format As Table.
4. Select one of the built-in formats from the drop-down menu, as shown in Figure 3.1.

FIGURE 3.1   Table styles in the Format As Table drop-down menu

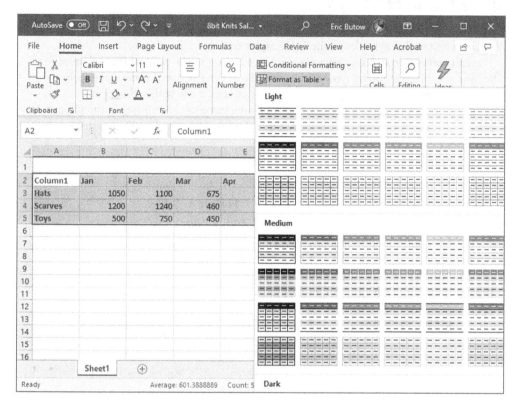

5. In the Format As Table dialog box (see Figure 3.2), select the My Table Has Headers check box if the cell range has no headers. Otherwise, proceed to step 6.

6. Leave the selected cells in the Where Is The Data box as it is and then click OK.

The selected cells are still selected, but now they sport the style of your new table.

FIGURE 3.2   Format As Table dialog box

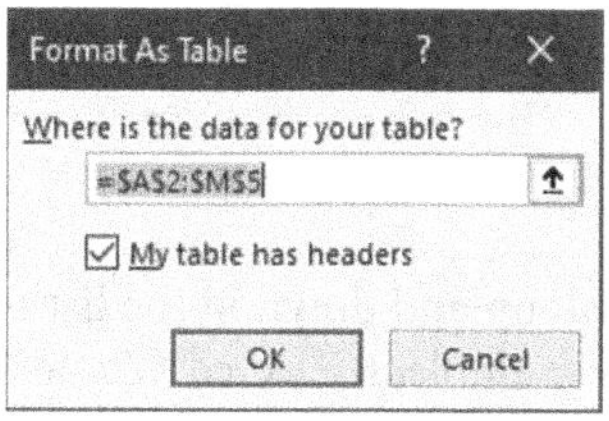

Applying Table Styles

After you create a table, the Table Design menu ribbon opens so that you can apply a style by clicking one of the style tiles in the Table Styles section in the ribbon.

You can view more styles by clicking the More button to the right of the style tiles row. (The More button is a down arrow with a line above it.) The list of styles appears in the drop-down menu you saw in Figure 3.1, so you can click a tile within the menu.

If none of the styles interests you, you can change some of the features in the table style or even create a style of your own. Follow these steps to create and apply a custom style to a table:

1. Click a cell in the table.
2. Click the Home menu option, if necessary.
3. In the Styles section in the Home ribbon, click Format As Table.
4. In the drop-down menu you saw in Figure 3.1, click New Table Style.
5. In the New Table Style dialog box, shown in Figure 3.3, press Backspace and then type the new style name in the Name box.

FIGURE 3.3 Highlighted default name in the New Table Style dialog box

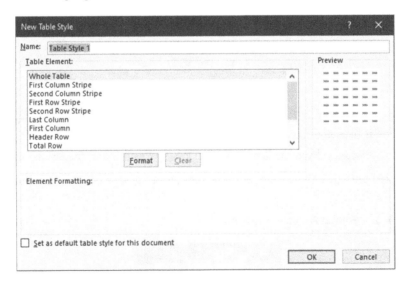

6. In the Table Element list, scroll up and down in the list to view all table elements, and then click an element. In this example, I selected Whole Table.
7. Click Format to open the Format Cells dialog box.
8. In the Format Cells dialog box, shown in Figure 3.4, you can change the font, border, and fill color and pattern by selecting the Font, Border, and Fill tabs, respectively.

FIGURE 3.4   Format Cells dialog box

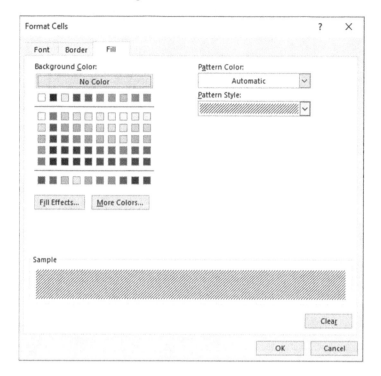

For this example, I selected the Fill tab, clicked the Thin Diagonal Strip pattern, and then clicked OK. The Preview area in the New Table Style dialog box shows all cells in the table with a gray background.

9. After you click OK, the table still looks the same in the worksheet. Now you have to repeat steps 1–3 and then select the custom table style from the drop-down menu in the Custom section.

You can only add a custom table style for all worksheets within one workbook. You cannot apply a custom table style in one workbook to another workbook.

Converting Tables to Cell Ranges

If you have a table and you think it would work better as a cell range in the worksheet instead, here's how to convert your table into a cell range:

1. Click a cell in the table.
2. Click the Table Design menu option.
3. In the Tools section in the Table Design ribbon, click Convert To Range, as shown in Figure 3.5.

FIGURE 3.5   Convert To Range menu option

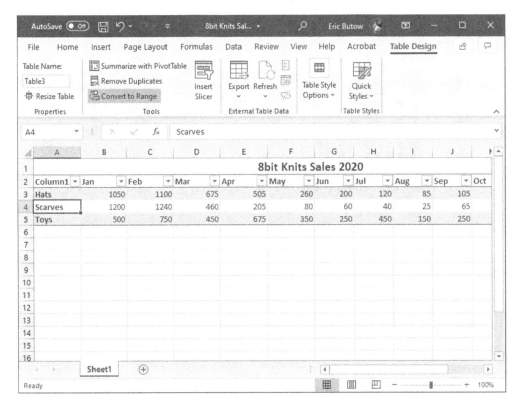

The table data appears in cells in the worksheet, but it keeps the same formatting. For example, if you have shading in the background of odd-numbered rows, the shading remains in those rows.

 Remember that when you convert a table back into a cell, you no longer have all the features of a table, including the ability to quickly filter columns.

EXERCISE 3.1

Creating a Table

1. Open an existing workbook.

2. Convert a range of cells into a table.

3. Apply a blue background style of your choice.

4. Convert the table back into a cell range.

Modifying Tables

After you create a table, you may want to modify it to meet your needs. However, you modify cells in a table differently than you do with cells in a worksheet. As with tables in Word, you can add or remove table rows and columns, change prebuilt or custom table styles you already applied to a table, and add what Excel calls a *total row* so that you can total values in table columns quickly.

Adding or Remove Table Rows and Columns

As with cells in a worksheet, a common task of working in a table is to add and remove table rows and/or columns so that the table contains and presents its information the way you want.

Add Table Rows and Columns

Add row(s) and/or column(s) to your table by following these steps:

1. Click a cell in the table.
2. Click the Table Design menu option.
3. In the Properties section in the Table Design ribbon, click Resize Table, as shown in Figure 3.6.
4. You can either resize the table to include the existing table plus any other rows that you want to add, or you can type the cell number into the Resize Table dialog box, as shown in Figure 3.7.
5. Click OK in the dialog box.

The added cells appear below and/or to the right of your existing table. If your table has any formatting applied to it, then the new cells within your table also reflect that formatting.

> If you don't select all the cells in your existing table along with the new cells that you want to add, a dialog box appears, stating that the range does not work because that range does not align with the existing table. Click OK to close the dialog box and select all the existing cells, as well as the new cells that you want to add.

Remove Table Rows and Columns

When you want to remove row(s) and/or column(s) from your table, follow these steps:

1. Select a cell within the table row or column you want to delete.
2. Click the Home menu option, if necessary.

3. In the Cells section in the Home ribbon, click the Delete icon as shown in Figure 3.8. (If your Excel window width is small, click the Cells icon and then click the Delete icon.)

4. Select Delete Table Rows or Delete Table Columns from the drop-down menu.

FIGURE 3.6   Resize Table option

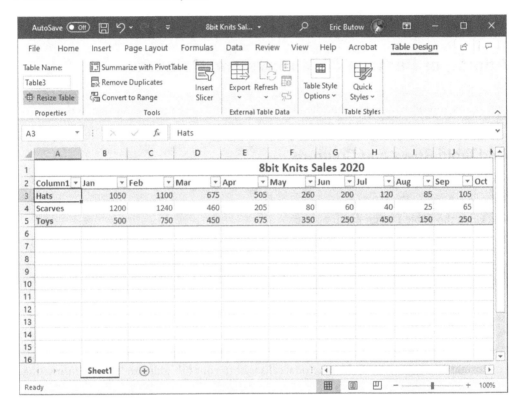

FIGURE 3.7   The reordered table rows

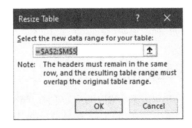

FIGURE 3.8   The Delete Table Rows and Delete Table Columns options

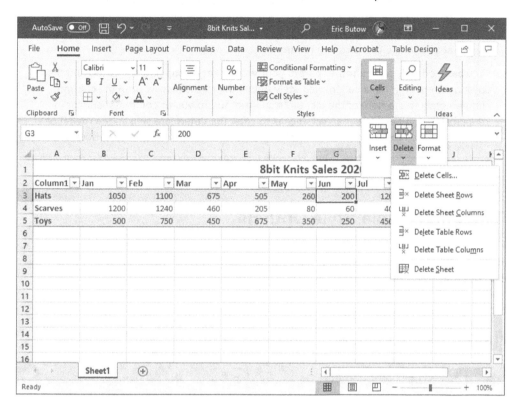

The row or column disappears from the table. If you need to get the row or column back, click the Undo icon in the Quick Access Toolbar on the left side of the Excel window title bar. You can also press Ctrl+Z.

Other Ways to Add and Remove Table Rows and Columns

Excel contains several other methods for removing rows and/or columns, depending on the circumstances:

- You can remove one or more duplicate columns by clicking in the table, clicking the Table Design menu option, and then clicking Remove Duplicates in the Tools section in the Table Design ribbon. In the Remove Columns dialog box, select the check box to the left of each column that you don't want to delete and then click OK. Excel promptly deletes the duplicated columns.

- Type in a cell within the column to the right of the last column in the table, or type in a cell within the row immediately below the last row of the table. After you finish typing and press Enter, Excel automatically adds a new row or column to the table with the text that you added in the row or column.

- You can add cells from another part of your worksheet by copying the cell(s) and then pasting them either in a cell immediately below the last table row or in the column immediately to the right of the last table column. The row(s) or column(s) appear in the table. If you have fewer selected cells to copy than there are cells in the row(s) or column(s), then Excel leaves the remaining cells in the new row(s) or column(s) blank.

Configuring Table Style Options

After you add a table, you may want to change how your table looks more quickly than having to create a new style, as you learned about earlier in this chapter. Start by clicking a cell in your table.

Next, click the Table Design menu option. The Table Style Options section, shown in Figure 3.9, contains seven check boxes that you can select to change how the table looks.

FIGURE 3.9   Table Style Options section check boxes

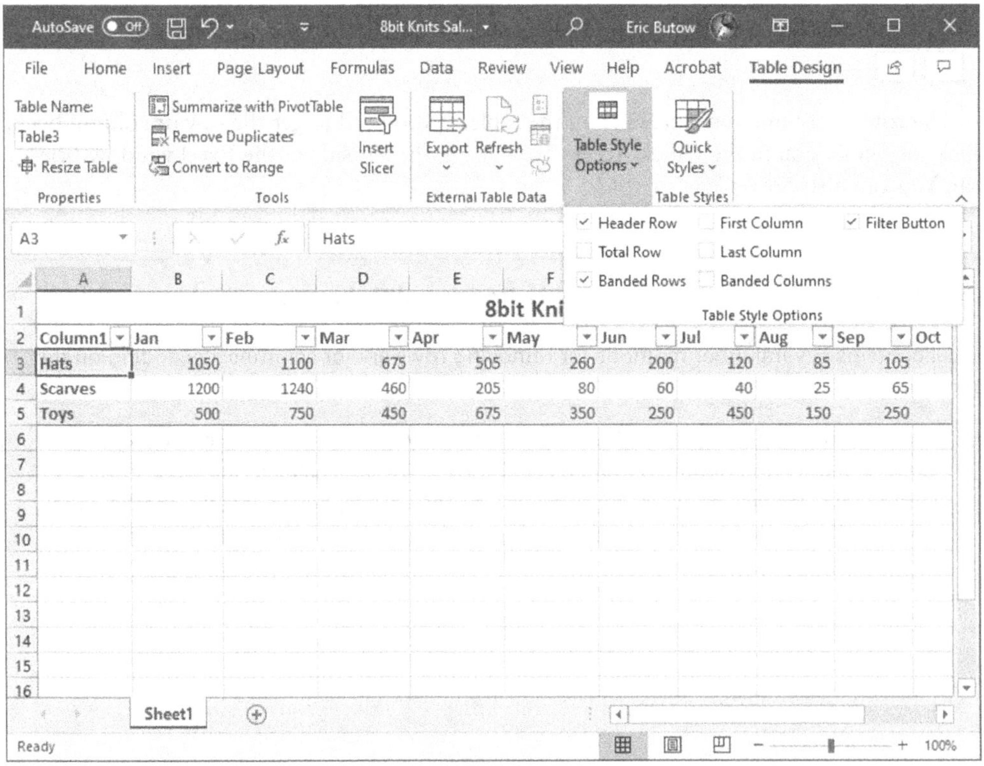

If your Excel window width is small, click the Table Style Options icon to view the drop-down list containing the seven check boxes.

Several of the check boxes are already checked to reflect the default Excel data style. You can click one of the following check boxes to turn the style off and on:

Header Row: Hide the header row.

Total Row: Add a total row, as you will learn about in the next section.

Banded Rows: Turn off shading in odd-numbered rows.

First Column: Apply the First Column style to the first column in the table.

Last Column: Apply the Last Column style to the last column in the table.

Banded Columns: Turn on shading in odd-numbered columns.

Filter Button: Hide the filter buttons within every column in the header row.

The style options that you choose apply to that table. Any new table that you create uses the default style options: Header Row, Banded Rows, and Filter Button.

Inserting and Configuring Total Rows

One big advantage of using a table instead of cells in a worksheet is when you have a lot of numbers and you need to total up those numbers. Instead of totaling numbers in each individual column, Excel lets you create a total row. Here's how:

1. Click a cell in the table.
2. Click the Table Design menu option.
3. In the Table Design ribbon, click the Total Row check box in the Table Style Options section, as shown in Figure 3.10. (If your Excel window width is small, click the Table Style Options icon to view the drop-down list containing the check box.)

The total row appears at the bottom of the table with the total of the numbers in the right column within the total row. However, numbers in your other columns are not totaled.

You can change that by clicking an empty cell within the total row, clicking the down arrow button to the right of the cell, and then selecting Sum from the drop-down menu (see Figure 3.11).

FIGURE 3.10   Total Row check box

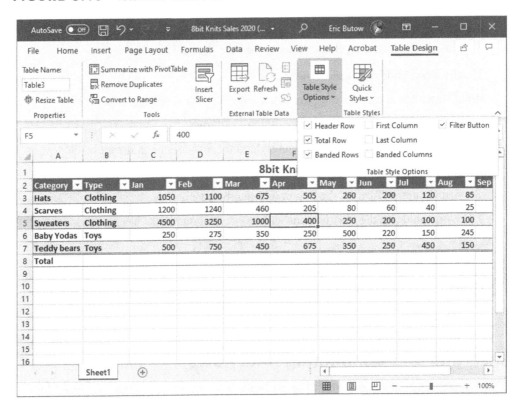

The total for all numbers in the column appears in the cell. If you want to display a different number instead of the total, you can select from one of the following options in the drop-down menu:

Average: The average of all numbers in the column

Count: The number of cells in the column, excluding the header row

Count Numbers: The number of cells that contains numbers within the column, excluding the header row

Max: The maximum number in the column

Min: The minimum number in the column

Sum: Totals all cells with numbers in the column

StdDev: The standard deviation of all numbers in the column

Var: The estimated variance based on all numbers in the column

FIGURE 3.11 Sum option in drop-down menu

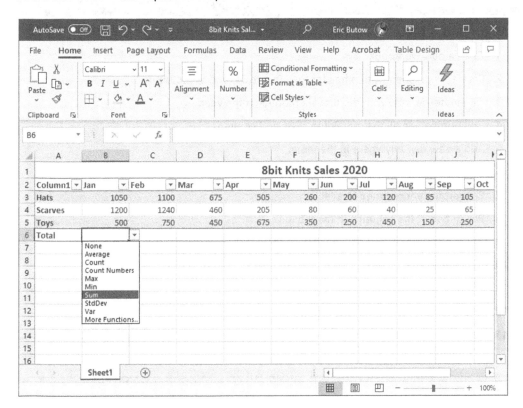

If you want to view more functions, select More Functions from the bottom of the drop-down list. Then you can view all the functions and select one in the Insert Functions dialog box, but that is beyond the scope of the exam.

One drawback of the total row is that you can't select cells in multiple columns and sum them all at the same time. Instead, after you total your first column, click and hold the mouse button down on the green box (called the fill handle) at the bottom-right corner of the selected cells. Then drag the mouse pointer to the left or right until you fill the cells that you want in the total row. When you release the mouse button, all the cells that you selected sum all the numbers in their columns.

EXERCISE 3.2

Modifying a Table

1. Open a new workbook.

2. Create a worksheet with a header row, five rows, and six columns.

3. Fill the header row with the first six months of the year.

4. Add numbers in all the remaining rows and columns.

5. Add a new row anywhere in the table.

6. Add numbers to all the cells in each column within the row.

7. Convert the entire range to a table.

8. Resize two of the columns in the table.

9. Apply banded columns to the table.

10. Add a table row.

11. Apply a total row.

12. Total the numbers in the first column.

13. Apply the total from the first column in the total row to the other empty cells in the total row.

Filtering and Sorting Table Data

Tables make it easier to filter and sort data compared to entering information into a worksheet. When you convert a cell range into a table, or you create a table from scratch, Excel automatically adds a header row with filter controls. Each filter control is a down arrow button at the right side of the selected cell within the header row. And, as when you enter data in a worksheet, Excel makes it easy to sort data in one or multiple columns.

Filtering Records

When you want to filter your table, start by clicking the down arrow to the right of the column within the header row. In the drop-down menu, shown in Figure 3.12, you see the data in all the cells within the column.

FIGURE 3.12   Filter drop-down menu

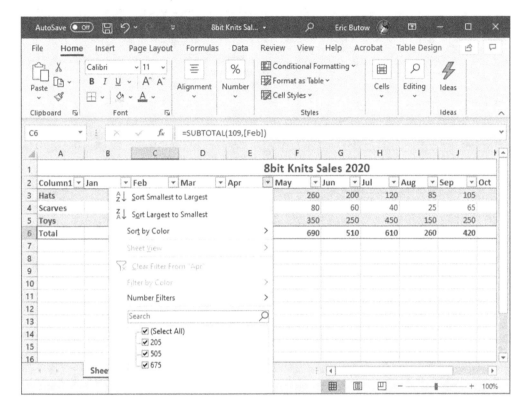

If you want to show only one or more cells within rows in your table, select the Select All check box to clear all the entries. Then you can click one or more check boxes to the left of the entry that you want to show in the table.

When you finish selecting the entry or entries, click OK. Excel filters the table so that it displays only the rows in the table that contain the cells you wanted to show within the column (see Figure 3.13).

The header row remains in the table, and if you have a total row, then the total row remains, too.

FIGURE 3.13   The filtered table shows one row that contains the cell.

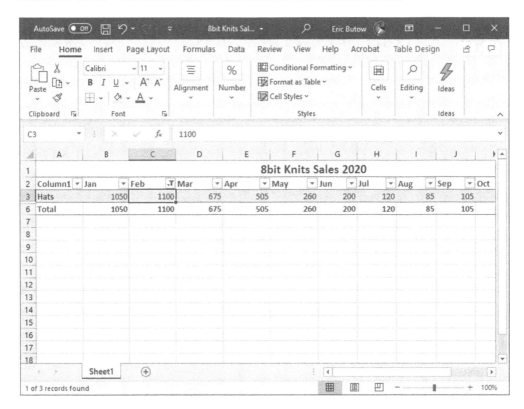

Real World Scenario

Filter Your Numbers Even More

Your boss has told you that she wants to filter your numbers even more than usual to high-light strong sales as part of her presentation to a big customer that she wants to land. That is, she wants the table to reflect all sales numbers that are at or above 10,000 sold, which conveniently happens to be all of the sales numbers for your company's most popular products during the past two quarters.

Fortunately, Excel makes it easy for you to set a filter to show numbers that are greater than, equal to, or less than a certain level. Set a numeric filter by following these steps:

1.   Click the Filter button in one of the column header rows.

2.   Move the mouse pointer over Number Filters in the drop-down menu.

3.   Click Greater Than Or Equal To.

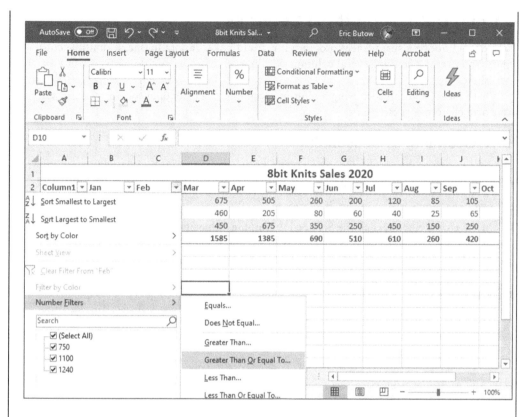

4. The cursor blinks in the top text box in the Custom AutoFilter dialog box so that you can type in the amount that you want to set.

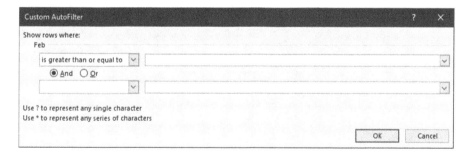

5. Click OK.

All of the rows that contain a number equal to or larger than 10,000 appear in the filtered table. You also see all the other columns within that row, so be careful; if one of the other columns in the row has a number lower than 10,000, that number will still show up in your table.

Sorting Data by Multiple Columns

Excel would not be a spreadsheet program if it could not sort data in one or multiple columns. You can sort cells in several columns within a table just as you do with cells in a worksheet.

What's more, you can sort using a built-in ascending or descending sort, or you can set your own custom sort criteria.

Sort Ascending or Descending

Sort cells in one or more columns in ascending or descending order by following these steps:

1. Select cells in at least two columns.
2. Click the Home menu option, if necessary.
3. In the Home ribbon, click the Sort & Filter in the Table Style Options section, as shown in Figure 3.14. (If your Excel window width is small, click the Editing icon and then click Sort & Filter.)

FIGURE 3.14 Sort & Filter drop-down menu

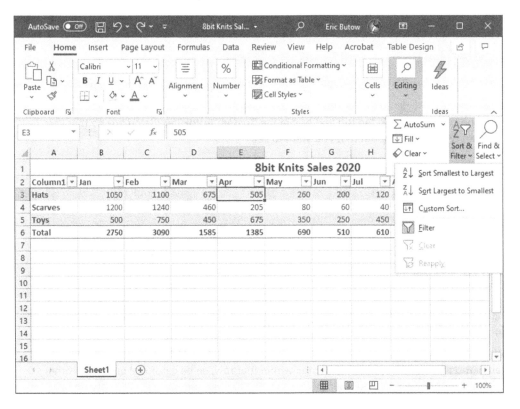

Now you can select from one of two built-in sort options in the drop-down menu:

Sort Smallest To Largest, or Sort A to Z: Sort the numbers in the column from smallest at the top to largest at the bottom if they're all numbers, or from A to Z if all the cells in the column have text.

Sort Largest To Smallest, or Sort Z to A: Sort the numbers in the column from largest at the top to smallest at the bottom if they're all numbers, or from Z to A if all the cells in the column have text.

When you sort from smallest to largest (or from A to Z), and vice versa, Excel sorts all the numbers or text within all the column(s).

 If you have a total row in your table, Excel sorts that cell, too. When you sort columns in the table with a total row, the total row will appear in a different row than the bottom, which will completely mess up your table totals.

Create a Custom Sort

If you need more control over what you want to sort, here's how to do that:

1. Select cells in at least two columns.
2. Click the Home menu option, if necessary.
3. In the Home ribbon, click Sort & Filter in the Table Style Options section, as you saw in Figure 3.14. (If your Excel window width is small, click the Editing icon and then click Sort & Filter.)
4. Select Sort Custom from the drop-down menu, as you saw in Figure 3.14.

Excel selects all the cells in your table. In the Sort dialog box shown in Figure 3.15, you can sort in one of three ways:

- By column in the Column box. The default selection is the first column in the table.
- By what you sort in the Sort On box, including the default cell values, the cell color, the font color, or a conditional format.
- The sort order in the Order box. You can also create a custom list to sort in nonsequential order, such as clothes sizes.

Click one of the three drop-down boxes to change how you sort. What you select in one box will affect what you see in other boxes. For example, if you sort by a column of text, you see A To Z in the Order box. If you sort by number, then you see Smallest To Largest in the Order box.

When you're done setting your custom sort, click OK. Excel reorders the rows based on the sort order within the column you selected.

FIGURE 3.15   Sort dialog box

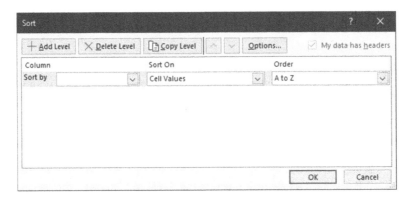

 If you select an even number of cells within the column, Excel will sort by the type (letter or number), depending on whether the majority of cells have text or numbers. What happens if you have the same number of cells with text and the same amount with numbers? Excel sorts the cells by letter.

EXERCISE 3.3

Filtering and Sorting Your Table Data

1. Open a new workbook.

2. Create a new table that has four rows (excluding the header row) and five columns.

3. Enter numbers into the non-header cells within the table.

4. Filter two of the columns so that they appear largest to smallest.

5. Sort two different columns so that they appear smallest to largest.

Summary

This chapter started by showing you how to create a table from a cell range. Then you learned how to apply table styles. You also learned how to create a cell range from an existing table.

After you learned about creating a table and applying table styles, I discussed how to modify tables further by adding and removing multiple rows and columns. Next, you learned how to modify the table style options within the Table Design menu ribbon. You also saw how to create a total row to create totals quickly within columns that have numbers in their cells.

Finally, you learned how to filter columns using the built-in table filter tool, as well as how to sort one or more columns in a table.

Key Terms

filter	tables
sort	total rows

Exam Essentials

Understand how to create tables from cell ranges, and vice versa. Know how to convert a table from a cell range in the Home menu ribbon and how to change a table into a cell range in the Table Design menu ribbon.

Know how to add and apply table styles. Understand how to apply prebuilt and custom table styles to a table, as well as how to apply styles quickly in the Table Design menu ribbon.

Understand how to modify tables. Know how to add and remove rows and columns, as well as insert and configure total rows.

Know how to filter records. Understand how to use the built-in filter function in a table to filter a column in ascending or descending letter order, smallest to largest number, or largest to smallest number.

Be able to sort data by multiple columns. Know how to sort multiple columns in a table in ascending or descending letter order, smallest to largest number, or largest to smallest number.

Review Questions

1. When you convert a table into a cell range, what happens to the table formatting?
    A. The formatting disappears.
    B. A dialog box appears that asks you if you want to keep your formatting.
    C. The formatting remains.
    D. A dialog box appears that warns you that if you go ahead with the conversion, you will lose all formatting.

2. How do you quickly get back a deleted row or column in a table? (Select all that apply.)
    A. Click Insert in the Home menu ribbon to insert the row or column again.
    B. Press Ctrl+Z.
    C. Resize the table.
    D. Click Undo in the Quick Access Toolbar.

3. In what order is a sort from the letters Z to A?
    A. Ascending
    B. Alphabetical
    C. Descending
    D. Backward

4. What formats can you change in a table style? (Choose all that apply.)
    A. Font
    B. Alignment
    C. Border
    D. Fill color and pattern

5. What is the difference between Count and Count Numbers?
    A. They both count the number of cells in the column.
    B. They both tell you how many cells have numbers in them.
    C. The Count feature includes all blank cells in the column.
    D. The Count Numbers feature counts how many cells have numbers.

6. What are the three default styles applied to a table? (Choose all that apply.)
    A. Filter Button
    B. Banded Rows
    C. Banded Columns
    D. Header Row

7. What features appear in a table after you create one from a cell range? (Choose all that apply.)

    A. Header row

    B. Filter button

    C. Banded columns

    D. Total row

8. What is the required sort criterion for a custom sort?

    A. Header row

    B. Sort On

    C. Column

    D. Order

9. What column does a total row total by default?

    A. The first column

    B. The last column

    C. Excel only puts the total row in but doesn't total any columns.

    D. All of the columns

10. Where do you apply a table style after you create it?

    A. In the Home menu ribbon

    B. In the Insert menu ribbon

    C. In the Page Layout menu ribbon

    D. In the Table Design menu ribbon

Chapter

4

Performing Operations by Using Formulas and Functions

MICROSOFT EXAM OBJECTIVES COVERED IN THIS CHAPTER:

✓ **Perform operations by using formulas and functions**

- Insert references

  - Insert relative, absolute, and mixed references

  - Reference named ranges and named tables in formulas

- Calculate and transform datas

  - Perform calculations by using the AVERAGE(), MAX(), MIN(), and SUM() functions

  - Count cells by using the COUNT(), COUNTA(), and COUNTBLANK() functions

  - Perform conditional operations by using the IF() function

- Format and modify text

  - Format text by using RIGHT(), LEFT(), and MID() functions

  - Format text by using UPPER(), LOWER(), and LEN() functions

  - Format text by using the CONCAT() and TEXTJOIN() functions

When you type a formula in a cell, Excel makes it easy to refer to specific cells and ranges. You can add one of three types of references: relative, absolute, and mixed. As you'll see in this chapter, Excel also allows you to refer to a cell range and a table within a workbook.

Next, I will show you how to perform simple calculations and operations using built-in calculation commands that you type into the Formula Bar. These include calculating the average, minimum, maximum, and sum of a group of cells that contain numbers, counting cells in selected cells or a range, and performing conditional operations with the IF() function.

Finally, you'll learn how to format and modify text in a cell by using a variety of functions. This includes how to return one or more characters at the right, left, or midpoint area with a text string; change text in a cell to uppercase and lowercase; display the number of characters in a text string; and combine text in different strings into one string.

Inserting References

Excel labels each cell with the column letter and then the row number, such as A5. This identification system makes it easy for you to refer to a cell when you enter a formula in another cell. For example, when you're in cell D9 and you want to multiply the number in cell D9 by 3, all you need to type is =(D9*3) in the *Formula Bar*.

You can create three different types of references:

Relative The default *relative cell reference* changes when you copy a formula from one cell into another cell. For example, if you type the formula =(D3*3) in cell D9 and then copy cell D9 to cell G9, Excel changes D3 in the formula to G3 because you are now in column G, as shown in the Formula Bar in Figure 4.1.

Absolute The *absolute cell reference* contains a dollar sign to the left of the letter and number in the cell that you reference, such as A5. When you add an absolute cell reference in a formula, the formula refers to a fixed point in the worksheet. For example, if you type the formula =(D3*3) in cell D9 and then copy cell D9 to cell G9, cell G9 still calculates the formula using cell D3 (see the Formula Bar in Figure 4.2).

Mixed A *mixed cell reference* contains a dollar sign to the left of the letter or number in the cell you reference, such as $A5. When you add a mixed cell reference in a formula, you specify that you want to refer to a value in a fixed column or row in a worksheet. For example, if you type the formula =($D3*3) in cell D9 and then copy cell D9 into cells D10 and D11, Excel multiplies the cells in cells D3, D4, and D5 and places those results in cells D9, D10, and D11, respectively (see Figure 4.3).

FIGURE 4.1   Relative cell reference

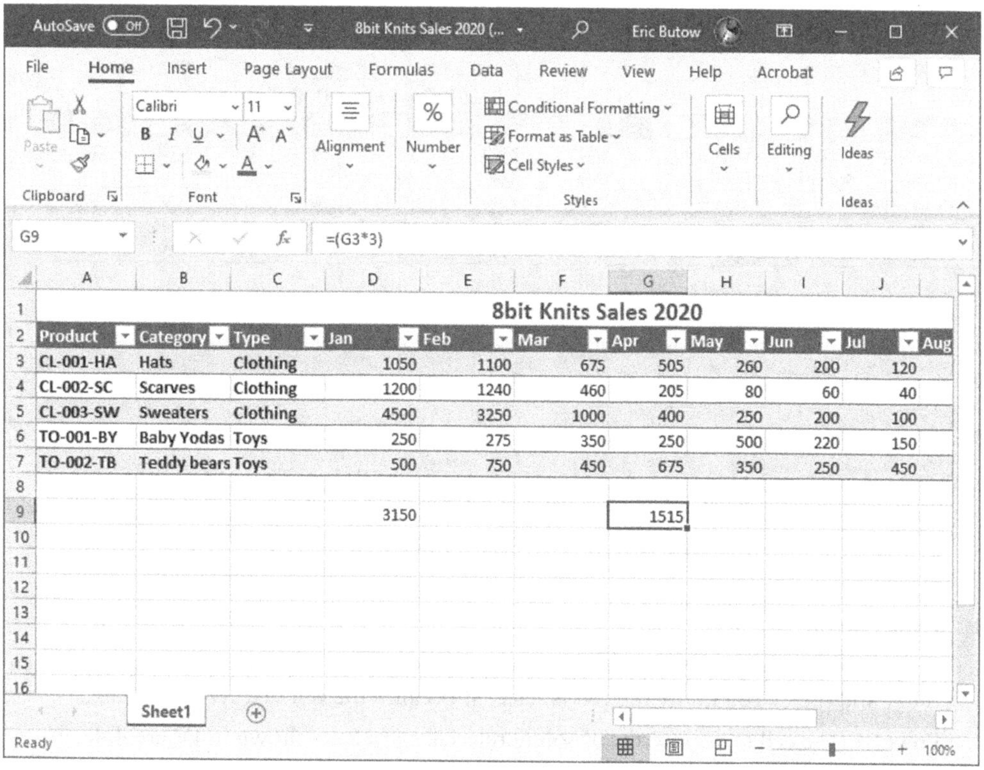

Inserting Relative, Absolute, and Mixed References

After you insert a reference into a formula, you may need to change the reference type from one type to another. Excel saves you some time by allowing you to change the reference type quickly. Here's how to do this:

1. Create a new workbook and add numbers to cells A1 through A4 in the worksheet.

2. In cell A6, type the formula =(A2*5) in the Formula Bar.

FIGURE 4.2   Absolute cell reference

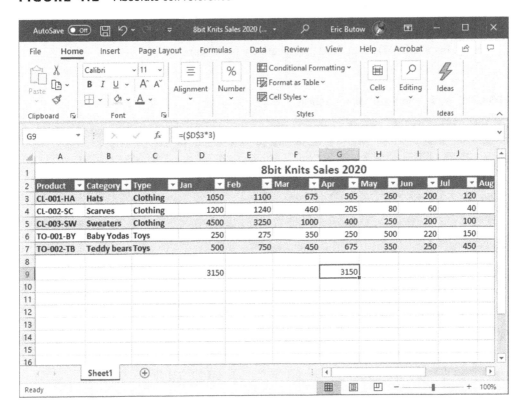

3. Press Enter.

4. In the Formula Bar, place the cursor to the left or right of A2 in the formula, or between the A and the 2. You know the cell is selected because the cell text A2 turns blue.

5. Press F4. The cell turns into the absolute reference A2, as shown in Figure 4.4.

6. Press F4 again. The cell turns into the mixed reference A$2.

7. Press F4 a third time. The cell turns into the mixed reference $A2.

8. Press F4 a final time to return the cell to its original relative reference A2.

9. Press Esc to exit the Formula Bar.

As you change each formula reference type in the Formula Bar, the new formula also appears in the cell.

FIGURE 4.3 Mixed cell reference

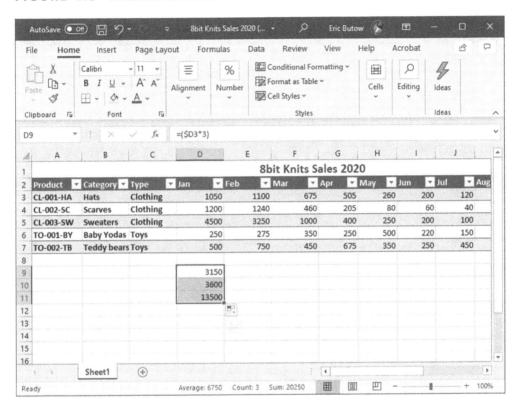

Referencing Named Ranges and Named Tables in Formulas

You don't need to use column names and numbers when you refer to cells in a formula. You can also refer to a named cell range or a named table within a formula. Here is an example that you can follow:

1. Open a workbook that has a cell range and a table with numeric values in a worksheet. If you don't have one, refer to previous chapters in this book to create a range and a table.

2. Click an empty cell below a column in the table.

3. In the Formula Bar, type **=SUM(** and then start typing the name of the table.

4. As you type, a list of potential matches appears in the drop-down list below the Formula Bar. Double-click the table name in the list.

FIGURE 4.4   Absolute reference in the Formula Bar

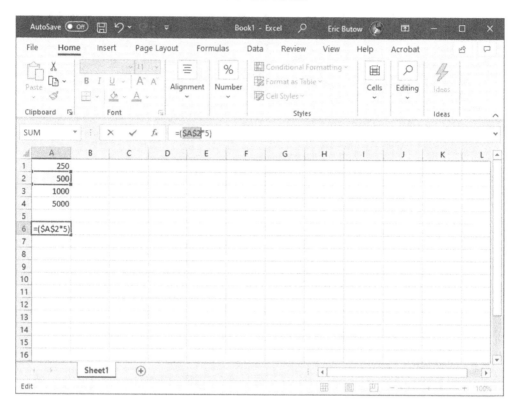

5. Now that the table name appears in the formula, start typing the name of the column in the table.

6. As you type, a list of potential matches appears in the drop-down list below the Formula Bar. Double-click the column name in the list.

7. Now that the column name appears in the formula, type) and then press Enter.

The total of all the numbers within the table appears in the cell, and Excel selects the cell directly below it. When you click the cell in the table, as shown in Figure 4.5, you see the formula in the Formula Bar.

If you need to check the name of the range or the table, click the down arrow at the right side of the Name Box, which appears to the left of the Formula Bar. Then click the name of the range or table. Excel highlights all the cells in the selected range or table. Now you can click the empty cell and add your formula using the range or table name.

FIGURE 4.5   The formula in the Formula Bar

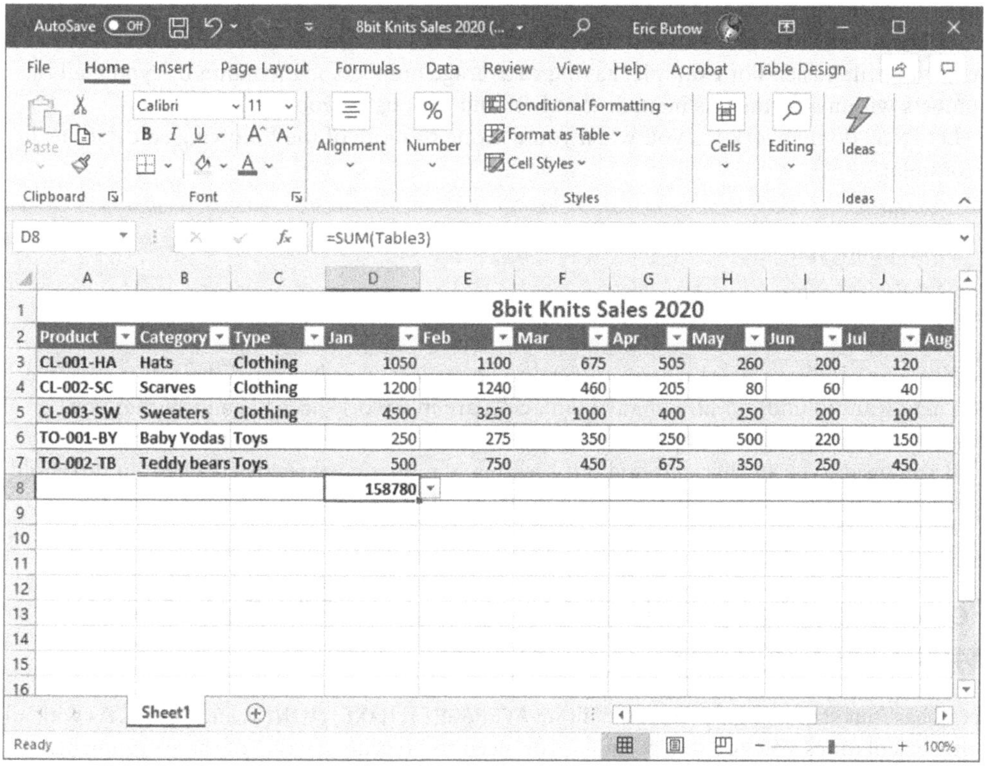

EXERCISE 4.1

Inserting References

1. Open a new worksheet.

2. Create a new table with four rows (with one header row) and four columns in the worksheet.

3. Label these columns Q1, Q2, Q3, and Q4.

4. Enter numbers in the cells within the table.

5. In cell A5, add a new formula that multiplies the amount in cell A2 by 4.

6. Move cell A5 to cell C5.

7. Change the formula in cell C5 to have an absolute reference to the cell.

8. Move cell C5 to cell B5.

9. Total the numbers in the name you have given to column D in the table.

Calculating and Transforming Datas

Excel includes a variety of built-in functions for calculating numbers in a spreadsheet to make your life easier. For example, having to average numbers in a column by typing all the numbers within a formula is inefficient at best and tedious at worst.

Let Excel do the work for you when you use one or more of the following calculations in a formula:

- Average
- Maximum value
- Minimum value
- Summation

You may also have times when you need to count instances in a worksheet. For example, you may want to find out how many blank cells are in a worksheet to confirm that you haven't missed adding any important data. Excel includes three counting functions.

If you need to go further and find out how many numeric values reach a certain threshold to meet a condition, such as where numbers are too hot or too cold, Excel includes the IF() function.

Performing Calculations Using the *AVERAGE()*, *MAX()*, *MIN()*, and *SUM()* Functions

Excel has four standard calculations built in: AVERAGE(), MAX(), MIN(), and SUM(). As with all other calculations you add to a formula, you need to precede any one of these arguments with the equal sign (=) in the Formula Bar.

AVERAGE()

The *average* is also known as the arithmetic mean, if you remember your middle school math. You can take the average of a group of cells in a worksheet, within a range, or within a table. You can also take an average of two numbers.

Average of Cells

In an empty cell, type **=AVERAGE** and then the cell range within the worksheet or table in parentheses. For example, if you type **=AVERAGE (D3:D7)** in the Formula Bar, as shown in the example in Figure 4.6, and then press Enter, the average of all five numbers in the column appears in the cell.

After you press Enter, Excel selects the cell directly below the cell with the average number. Click the cell with the average number to view the formula in the Formula Bar.

Average of Numbers

You can average as few as two or as many as 255 numbers by typing **=AVERAGE** and then entering up to 255 numbers within the parentheses. For example, if you

FIGURE 4.6   The average of all five numbers

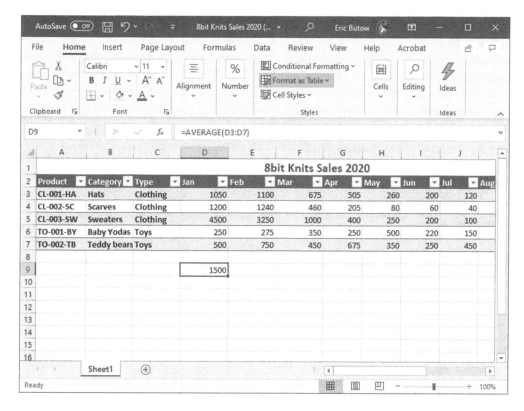

type **=AVERAGE(1,10,40,100,400)** in the Formula Bar (see Figure 4.7) and then press Enter, the average of all five numbers appears in the cell.

As you work with the AVERAGE() function, keep the following in mind:

- As you start typing **AVERAGE** in the Formula Bar, you see a drop-down list that shows functions that Excel thinks you want to add. If you would rather not finish typing the function, double-click AVERAGE in the list to add AVERAGE(to the Formula Bar.

- If you average cells within a range where a cell contains text, such as the text in a table header, then Excel does not include the information in those cells when it calculates the average.

- If one or more cells that you want to average contain errors, then the average will also return an error message.

- If you average cells within a range where a cell contains the number 0, then Excel includes that number in the average. However, if a cell in the range is empty, then Excel ignores that cell when it calculates the average.

FIGURE 4.7   Average of five numbers in the cell

Product	Category	Type	Jan	Feb	Mar	Apr	May	Jun	Jul	Aug
					8bit Knits Sales 2020					
CL-001-HA	Hats	Clothing	1050	1100	675	505	260	200	120	
CL-002-SC	Scarves	Clothing	1200	1240	460	205	80	60	40	
CL-003-SW	Sweaters	Clothing	4500	3250	1000	400	250	200	100	
TO-001-BY	Baby Yodas	Toys	250	275	350	250	500	220	150	
TO-002-TB	Teddy bears	Toys	500	750	450	675	350	250	450	

C9 =AVERAGE(1,10,40,100,400)

C9 value: 110.2

Real World Scenario

Use Averages for Different Criteria

Your boss has come to you with a request for the next company sales meeting. She wants you to show the average sales greater than $1,000 during the first quarter of the year. Then she wants to show the average sale for months that have brought in more than $1,000 but less than $4,000.

Excel gives you two functions for doing these tasks quickly: AVERAGEIF() and AVERAGEIFS(). The difference between the two? AVERAGEIF() finds averages that meet one criterion, and AVERAGEIFS() finds averages that meet every one of the multiple criteria you specify in the argument.

Here's how to use both of these functions to calculate what your boss wants to see:

1. Select the cell below the range or the table where you want to display the average for the first quarter.

2. Type **=AVERAGEIF(D3:F7, ">1000")** in the Formula Bar.

3. Press Enter to view the average in the cell, as shown in the following graphic.

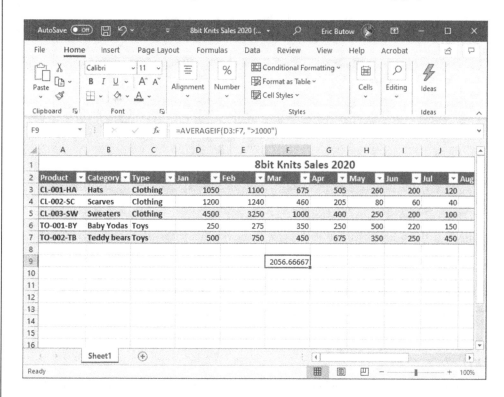

4. Select the cell below the range or the table where you want to display the average for the quarter.

5. Type **=AVERAGEIFS(M3:O7,M3:O7,">1000",M3:O7,"<4000")** in the Formula Bar.

6. Press Enter to view the average in the cell.

7. Click the cell again to view the formula in the cell, as shown in the following graphic:

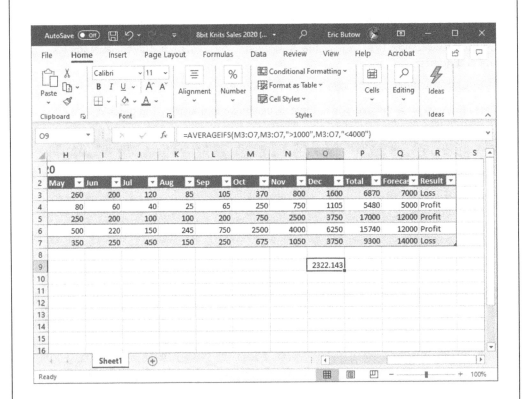

Note that if a selected cell is empty, then Excel treats the cell as including the number 0.

MAX()

If you need to find the largest number in a range of cells or cells within a table, the MAX() function is the tool you need. After you select a blank cell to add the formula, you can add the MAX() function in the Formula Bar in one of two ways:

- Type =MAX(a,b,c . . .), where a, b, c, and so on are numbers of your choosing. You can add as many as 255 numbers. When you finish typing the formula, press Enter to see the result in the cell.

- Type =MAX(and then select a range of cells in the worksheet or the table. Excel automatically adds the cell range in your worksheet, so all you have to do is type) to close the formula and then press Enter. You can see the result in the cell shown in Figure 4.8.

FIGURE 4.8   The calculated MAX result in the cell and the formula in the Formula Bar

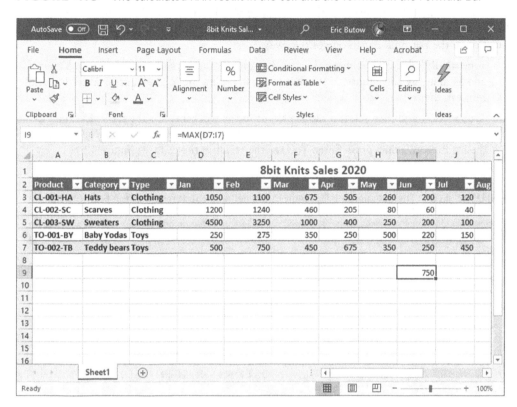

Keep the following in mind when you work with the MAX() function:

- As you start typing **MAX** in the Formula Bar, you see a drop-down list that shows functions that Excel thinks you want to add to the formula. If you would rather not finish typing the function, double-click MAX in the list to add MAX(to the Formula Bar.

- If you calculate the maximum number of cells within a range where a cell contains text, such as the text in a table header, then Excel does not include the information in those cells when it calculates the maximum.

- If one or more cells that you selected contain errors, then the maximum calculation will also return an error message in the cell.

- If a cell in the range is empty, then Excel ignores that cell when it calculates the maximum.

MIN()

If you need to find the smallest number in a range of cells or cells within a table, use the MIN() function. After you select a blank cell to add the formula, you can add the MIN() function in the Formula Bar in one of two ways:

- Type =MIN(a,b,c . . .), where a, b, c, and so on are numbers of your choosing. You can add as many as 255 numbers. When you finish typing the formula, press Enter to see the result in the cell.

- Type =MIN(and then select a range of cells in the worksheet or the table. Excel automatically adds the cell range in your worksheet, so all you have to do is type) to close the formula and then press Enter. You see the result in the cell (see Figure 4.9).

FIGURE 4.9   The calculated MIN result in the cell and the formula in the Formula Bar

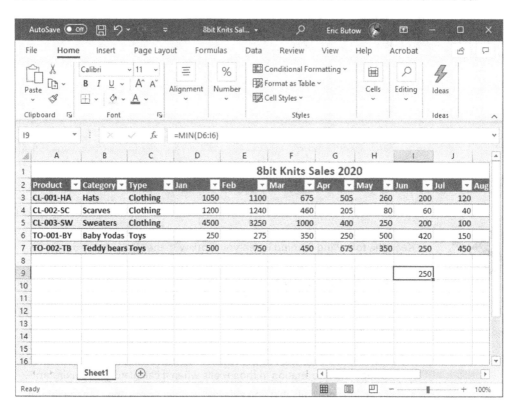

Keep the following in mind when you work with the MIN() function:

- As you start typing **MIN** in the Formula Bar, you see a drop-down list that shows functions that Excel thinks you want to add to the formula. If you would rather not finish typing the function, double-click MIN in the list to add MIN(to the Formula Bar.

- If you calculate the minimum number of cells within a range where a cell contains text, such as the text in a table header, then Excel does not include the information in those cells when it calculates the minimum.

- If one or more cells that you selected contain errors, then the minimum calculation will also return an error message in the cell.

- If a cell in the range is empty, then Excel ignores that cell when it calculates the minimum.

SUM()

When you need to summarize numbers or, more often, numbers in a range of cells, Excel makes this task easy with the SUM() function. After you select a blank cell to add the formula, you can add the SUM() function in the Formula Bar in one of three ways:

- Type =SUM(A1:A5), where you can replace A1:A5 with the starting and ending cells that you want to sum.

- You can sum multiple ranges of cells by typing commas between cell ranges, such as =SUM(A1:A5,D1:D5). When you finish typing the formula, press Enter to see the result in the cell.

- Type =SUM(and then select a range of cells in the worksheet or the table. Excel automatically adds the cell range in your worksheet, so all you have to do is type) to close the formula and then press Enter. You can see the result in the cell shown in Figure 4.10.

Counting Cells Using the *COUNT()*, *COUNTA()*, and *COUNTBLANK()* Functions

When you need to know how many cells in a worksheet or table have numbers, cells that are not empty, or cells that are empty, you don't have to go through a worksheet or table and count them yourself. You can use the three built-in counting functions.

FIGURE 4.10   The calculated SUM result in the cell and the formula in the Formula Bar

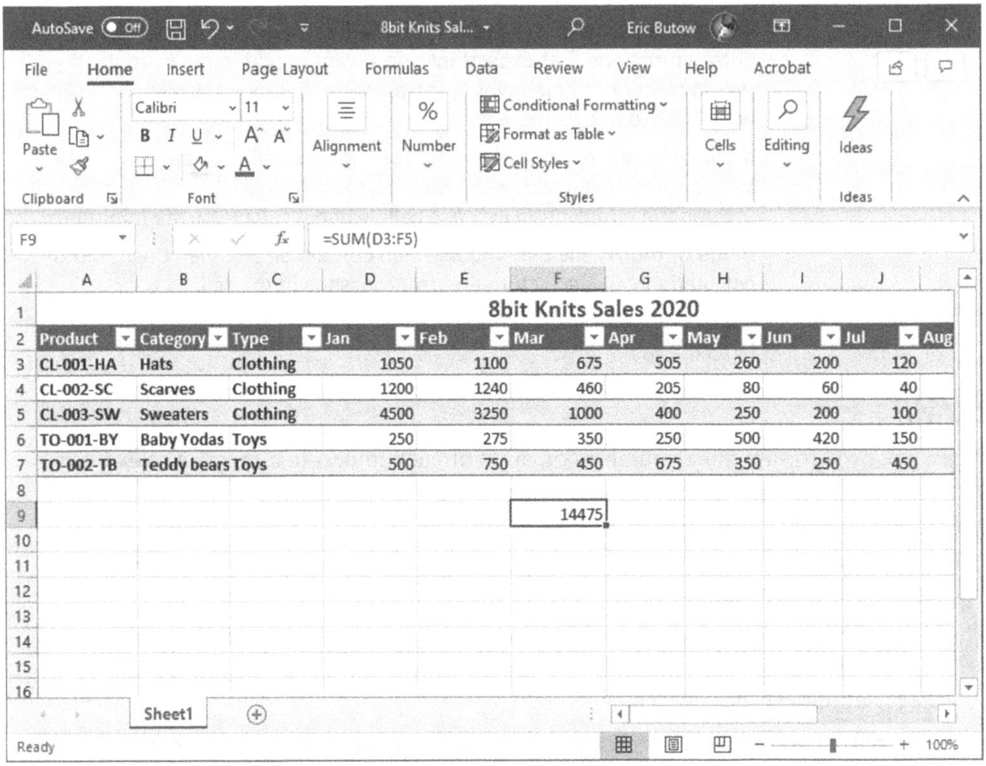

COUNT()

If you need to count how many cells in a range or cells within a table have numbers, use the COUNT() function. After you select a blank cell to add the formula, you can add the COUNT() function in the Formula Bar in one of three ways:

- Type =COUNT(a,b,c . . .), where a, b, c, and so on are numbers of your choosing. You can add as many as 255 numbers. When you finish typing the formula, press Enter to see the result in the cell.

- Type =COUNT(A1:A5), where you can replace A1:A5 with the starting and ending cells that you want to count.

- Type =COUNT(and then select a range of cells in the worksheet or the table. Excel automatically adds the cell range in your worksheet, so all you have to do is type) to close the formula and then press Enter. You can see the result in the cell shown in Figure 4.11.

FIGURE 4.11 The count result in the cell and the formula in the Formula Bar

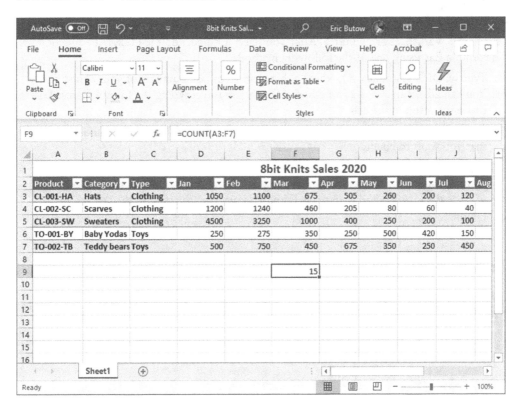

Keep the following in mind when you work with the COUNT() function:

- As you start typing **COUNT** in the Formula Bar, you see a drop-down list that shows functions that Excel thinks you want to add to the formula. If you would rather not finish typing the function, double-click COUNT in the list to add COUNT(to the Formula Bar. Then you can select or type the range, type), and then press Enter.

- Excel counts cells with numbers, dates, and even a text representation of numbers such as the number 5 in quotes ("5").

- If one or more cells that you selected contain errors, then the count will also return an error message in the cell.

- If a cell in the range is empty, then Excel ignores that cell during the count.

COUNTA()

You can use the COUNTA() function to count the number of cells that are not empty within a range in a worksheet or in a table. After you select a range, add the COUNTA() function in the Formula Bar using one of the following methods:

- Type =COUNTA(a,b,c . . .), where a, b, c, and so on are numbers of your choosing. You can add as many as 255 numbers. When you finish typing the formula, press Enter to see the result in the cell.

- Type =COUNTA(E1:E5) where you can replace E1:E5 with the starting and ending cells that you want to count.

- Type =COUNT(and then select a range of cells in the worksheet or the table. Excel automatically adds the cell range in your worksheet, so all you have to do is type) to close the formula and then press Enter. You can see the result in the cell shown in Figure 4.12.

FIGURE 4.12   The COUNTA results in the cell and the formula in the Formula Bar

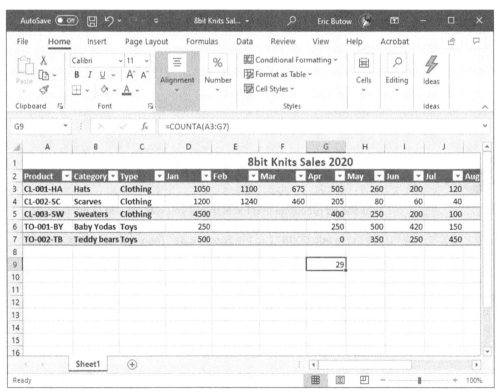

When you use the COUNTA() function, note the following:

- As you start typing **COUNTA** in the Formula Bar, you see a drop-down list that shows functions that Excel thinks you want to add to the formula. If you would rather not finish typing the function, double-click COUNTA in the list to add COUNTA(to the Formula Bar. Then you can select or type the range, type), and then press Enter.
- The COUNTA() function counts all cells with any type of information including cells that contain errors.
- If a cell in the range is empty, then Excel ignores that cell when it calculates the maximum.

COUNTBLANK()

The COUNTBLANK() function counts the number of empty cells within a selected range in a worksheet or table.

Once you select the range, add the COUNTBLANK() function in the Formula Bar by typing **=COUNTBLANK(** and then type the cell range, or you can select a range of cells in the worksheet or the table. Excel automatically adds the cell range in your worksheet, so all you have to do is type) to close the formula and then press Enter. You can see the result in the cell shown in Figure 4.13.

Keep the following in mind when you work with the COUNTBLANK() function:

- As you start typing **COUNTBLANK** in the Formula Bar, you see a drop-down list that shows functions that Excel thinks you want to add to the formula. If you would rather not finish typing the function, double-click COUNTBLANK in the list to add COUNTBLANK(to the Formula Bar. Then you can select or type the range, type), and then press Enter.
- If you type the number 0 in a cell, Excel considers that cell to be populated.

Perform Conditional Operations by Using the *IF()* Function

If you've ever taken a computer programming class or even used a spreadsheet program before, you know that the if-then operation is one of the basic operations that you can use to find out if text or a numerical value is true or false.

You can easily add an if-then condition to a cell in a worksheet or table by using the IF() function. There are two ways to compare values using the IF() function: by having Excel tell you if a cell contains text or a number or if a numeric value meets the condition.

FIGURE 4.13 The calculated COUNTBLANK result in the cell and formula in the Formula Bar

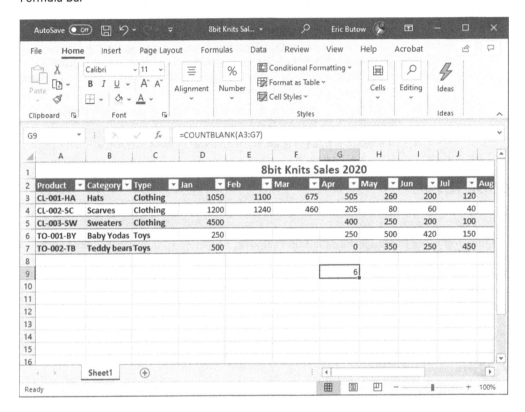

Show if a Cell Contains Text

Here's how to have Excel tell you if a cell contains the text you want to show:

1. Place the cursor in cell C9.

2. Type **=IF(C7="Clothing",true,false)** in the Formula Bar.

3. Press Enter.

   Excel shows FALSE within the cell, as shown in Figure 4.14.

The TRUE or FALSE result appears in all uppercase letters whether or not you capitalize some or all of the words "true" and "false" in the formula.

FIGURE 4.14   The FALSE result in the cell with the formula in the Formula Bar

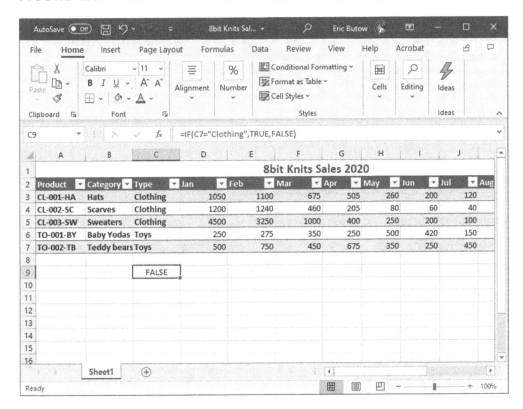

Show if the Numeric Value Meets the Condition

To show that a numeric value meets a certain condition, such as the value in one cell being smaller than another, follow these steps:

1. Click cell R3 in the table.

2. Type =IF(P3<Q3,"Loss","Profit") in the Formula Bar. In this formula, Loss is the condition if the comparison is true, and Profit is the condition if the comparison is false.

3. Press Enter.

   In the table, Excel shows results not only in cell R3 but also within all cells within column R (see Figure 4.15).

   Excel copied the formula into all cells, so now you can see if all of the totals in column O when compared with the forecast numbers in column P resulted in a loss or profit for the year.

FIGURE 4.15 The results of the formula in column R

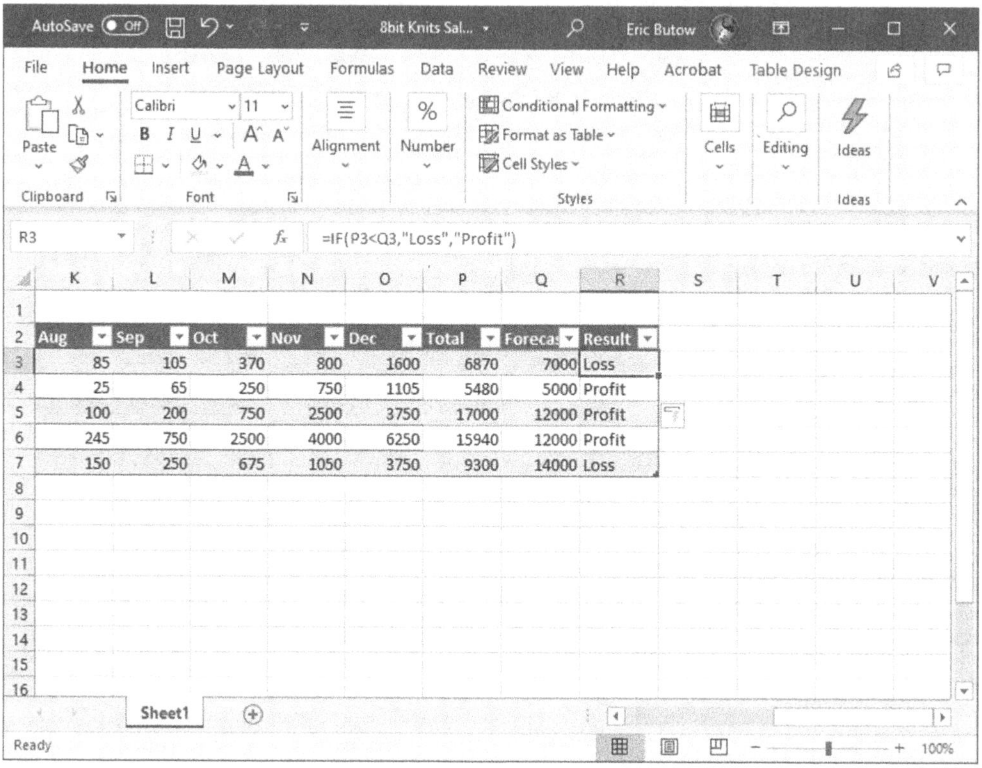

EXERCISE 4.2

Calculate and Transform Datas

1. Open a new document.
2. Add a new table with five columns and six rows.
3. Populate the table with numbers.
4. In column F, summarize all the numbers within each row.
5. In cell A7, view the maximum number of all the numbers in the column.
6. In cell B7, view the minimum number of all the numbers in the column.
7. In cell C7, count all the cells in the column.
8. In cell F7, have Excel report if cell F6 is greater than cell F1.

Formatting and Modifying Text

Lists are an effective way of presenting information that readers can digest easily, as demonstrated in this book. Excel includes many powerful tools to create lists easily and then format them so that they look the way you want them to appear.

Formatting Text Using the *RIGHT()*, *LEFT()*, and *MID()* Functions

When you need to extract specific characters from text to place it in another cell, such as only to show a prefix for a part name, you can do so by using the built-in RIGHT(), LEFT(), and MID() functions that you can add within a formula.

RIGHT()

The RIGHT() function shows the last characters in a string of text within a cell in a worksheet or table. Here's how to use the RIGHT() function in a cell:

1. Click cell A9 in the table.
2. Type **=RIGHT(A4,2)** in the Formula Bar. A4 is the cell and 2 is the number of characters to show in cell A9.
3. Press Enter.

The last two letters in cell A4 appear in cell A9, as shown in Figure 4.16.

Keep the following in mind when you work with the RIGHT() function:

- As you start typing **RIGHT** in the Formula Bar, you see a drop-down list that shows functions that Excel thinks you want to add to the formula. If you would rather not finish typing the function, double-click RIGHT in the list to add RIGHT(to the Formula Bar. Then you can select or type the range, type), and then press Enter.

- Excel considers spaces as characters.

- If you don't add a number after the cell within the formula, such as RIGHT(A4), then Excel will return only the last character in cell A4.

- You can also add a string of characters instead of the cell within a formula, such as **RIGHT("Microsoft Excel",5)** to display the characters Excel in the cell where you added the formula.

- If you specify a number of characters in the formula greater than the number of characters within the cell, then the formula counts all the characters.

- Excel does not support the RIGHT() function in all languages, so if this function does not work, contact Microsoft to determine whether Excel supports this function for your language.

FIGURE 4.16   The last two letters in cell A4

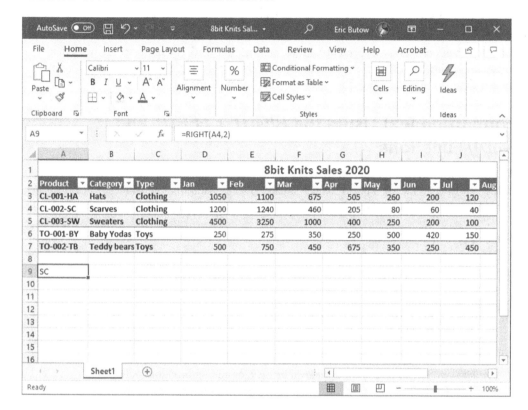

LEFT()

The LEFT() function shows the first characters in a string of text within a cell in a worksheet or table. Use the LEFT() function as demonstrated in the following example:

1. Click on cell A10 in the table.

2. Type =LEFT(A6,2) in the Formula Bar. A6 is the cell and 2 is the number of characters to show in cell A10.

3. Press Enter.

    The first two letters in cell A6 appear in cell A10 (see Figure 4.17).

FIGURE 4.17 The first two letters in cell A6

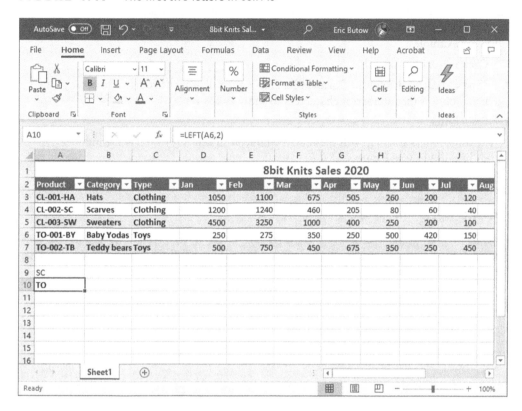

When you work with the LEFT() function, take note of the following:

- As you start typing **LEFT** in the Formula Bar, you see a drop-down list that shows the functions that Excel thinks you want to add to the formula. If you would rather not finish typing the function, double-click LEFT in the list to add LEFT(to the Formula Bar. Then you can select or type the range, type), and then press Enter.

- Excel considers spaces as characters.

- If you don't add a number after the cell within the formula, such as LEFT(A6), then Excel will return only the first character in cell A6.

- You can also add a string of characters instead of the cell within a formula, such as **LEFT("Microsoft Excel",5)** to display the characters Micro in the cell where you added the formula.

- If you specify a number of characters in the formula greater than the number of characters within the cell, then the formula counts all the characters.

- Excel does not support the LEFT() function in all languages, so if this function does not work, contact Microsoft to determine whether Excel supports this function for your language.

MID()

The MID() function shows a specific number of characters in a string of text within a cell in a worksheet or table. Follow these steps to use the MID() function, as shown in the following example:

1. Click cell A11 in the table.

2. Type =MID(A7,4,3) in the Formula Bar. A6 is the cell, 4 is the fourth character in the text, and 3 is the number of characters to show in cell A11.

3. Press Enter.

The three letters starting with the fourth character in cell A7, which is the number 0, appear in cell A11 (see Figure 4.18).

FIGURE 4.18   The three characters in cell A11

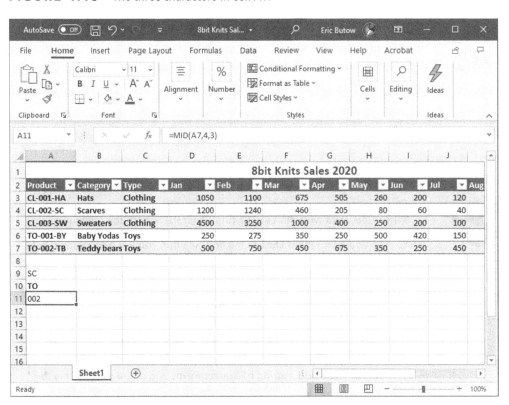

Here's more about what you need to be aware of when you work with the MID() function:

- As you start typing **MID** in the Formula Bar, you see a drop-down list that shows functions that Excel thinks you want to add to the formula. If you would rather not finish typing the function, double-click MID in the list to add MID(to the Formula Bar. Then you can select or type the range, type), and then press Enter.

- Excel considers spaces as characters.

- If you put the starting number in a location that is greater than the number of characters, then Excel simply returns no result. For example, the formula MID(D4,15,5) refers to cell D4 with only 11 characters in it, so the cell with the MID() formula shows nothing.

- If the number of characters that you want to show exceeds the number of characters, then Excel shows all the characters through the end of the text. For example, the formula MID(D4,5,10) refers to cell D4 with only 10 characters in it, so the cell with the MID() formula shows the last 6 characters of text.

- You can also add a string of characters instead of the cell within a formula, such as **MID ("Microsoft Excel",6,4)** to display the characters soft in the cell where you added the formula.

- If you specify a number of characters in the formula greater than the number of characters within the cell, then the formula counts all the characters.

- Excel does not support the MID() function in all languages, so if this function does not work, contact Microsoft to determine whether Excel supports this function for your language.

Formatting Text Using the *UPPER()*, *LOWER()*, and *LEN()* Functions

When you need to change the text in a cell to all uppercase or all lowercase letters, especially in multiple cells, then that task becomes tedious in no time. Excel has two built-in features for converting all text in cells within a worksheet or table to uppercase or lowercase.

UPPER()

The UPPER() function converts all text in one or more cells to uppercase. Follow these steps to use the UPPER() function:

1. Insert a new column to the left of column C.
2. Select cell C3.
3. Type =UPPER(B3) in the Formula Bar.
4. Press Enter.

Excel copies the formula into all cells in column C, so now all text in column B is uppercase in column C (see Figure 4.19).

FIGURE 4.19   All uppercase text in column C

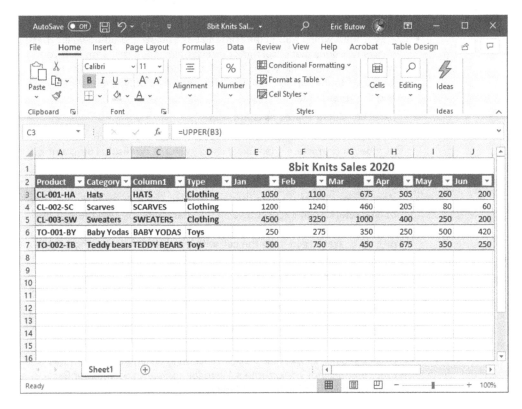

There are two things to know about using the UPPER() function:

- You can type a text string within the formula instead of a cell reference, such as **=UPPER("Excel")**, in the Formula Bar. If you add the formula within a table cell, then all cells in the column display EXCEL.

- If you have characters in your text that are numbers or special characters, Excel does not change them. For example, if you have the number 7, Excel does not change the 7 to &.

LOWER()

The LOWER() function converts all text in one or more cells to lowercase. Here's how to use the LOWER() function:

1. Insert a new column to the left of column C.
2. Select cell C3.
3. Type **=LOWER(B3)** in the Formula Bar.
4. Press Enter.

Excel copies the formula into all cells in column C, so now all text in column B is lowercase in column C (see Figure 4.20).

FIGURE 4.20 All lowercase text in column C

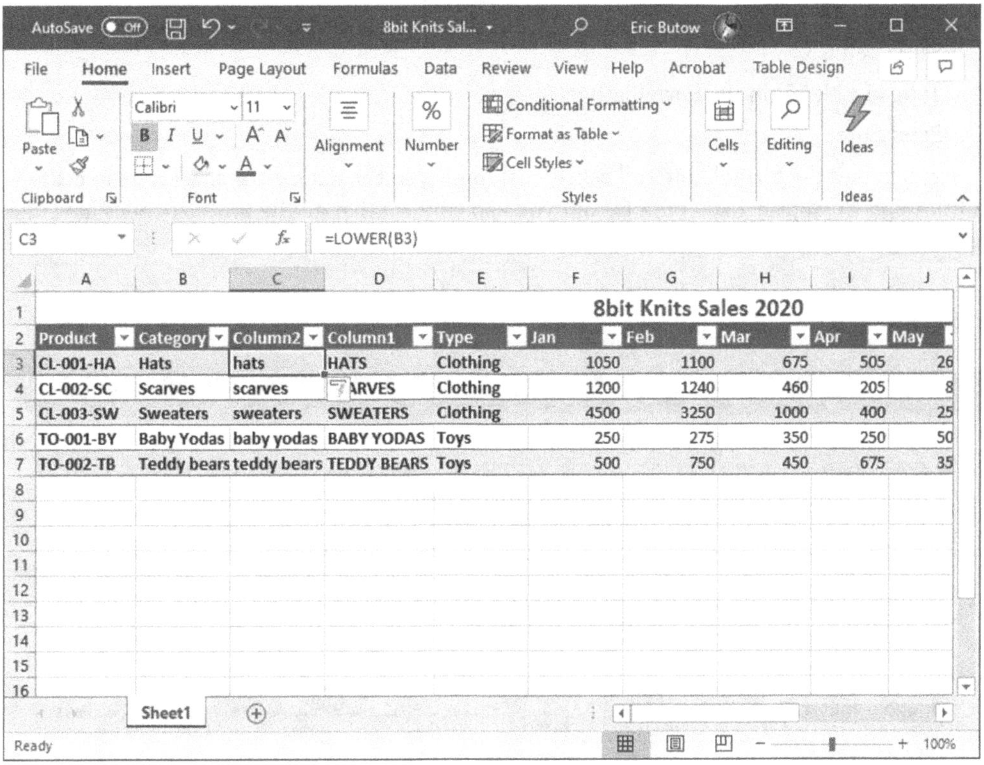

AutoSave Off
8bit Knits Sal...
Eric Butow
File Home Insert Page Layout Formulas Data Review View Help Acrobat Table Design
Calibri 11
Paste
Alignment
Number
Conditional Formatting
Format as Table
Cell Styles
Cells
Editing
Ideas
Clipboard
Font
Styles
Ideas
C3
=LOWER(B3)
8bit Knits Sales 2020
Product Category Column2 Column1 Type Jan Feb Mar Apr May
CL-001-HA Hats hats HATS Clothing 1050 1100 675 505 26
CL-002-SC Scarves scarves ARVES Clothing 1200 1240 460 205 8
CL-003-SW Sweaters sweaters SWEATERS Clothing 4500 3250 1000 400 25
TO-001-BY Baby Yodas baby yodas BABY YODAS Toys 250 275 350 250 50
TO-002-TB Teddy bears teddy bears TEDDY BEARS Toys 500 750 450 675 35
Sheet1
Ready
100%

NOTE

Here is some more information you should know about the `LOWER()` function:

- You can type a text string within the formula instead of a cell reference, such as **=LOWER("Excel")** in the Formula Bar. If you add the formula within a table cell, then all cells in the column display `excel`.
- If you have characters in your text that are numbers or special characters, Excel does not change them. For example, if you have the % symbol in the text, Excel does not change the % to 5.

LEN()

The LEN() function, which is short for length, tells you how many characters are in a text string within a cell. For example, you may need to have exactly 14 characters in a product code, and you want to find out which product code has too many or too few characters.

Add the LEN() function in a cell by following these steps:

1. Insert a new column to the left of column C.
2. Select cell C3.
3. Type **=LEN(A3)** in the Formula Bar.
4. Press Enter.

Excel copies the formula into all cells in column C, so the number of characters in cells A3 through A7 appear in column C, and you can confirm that all the product codes have the same length (see Figure 4.21).

FIGURE 4.21   Length in characters in column C

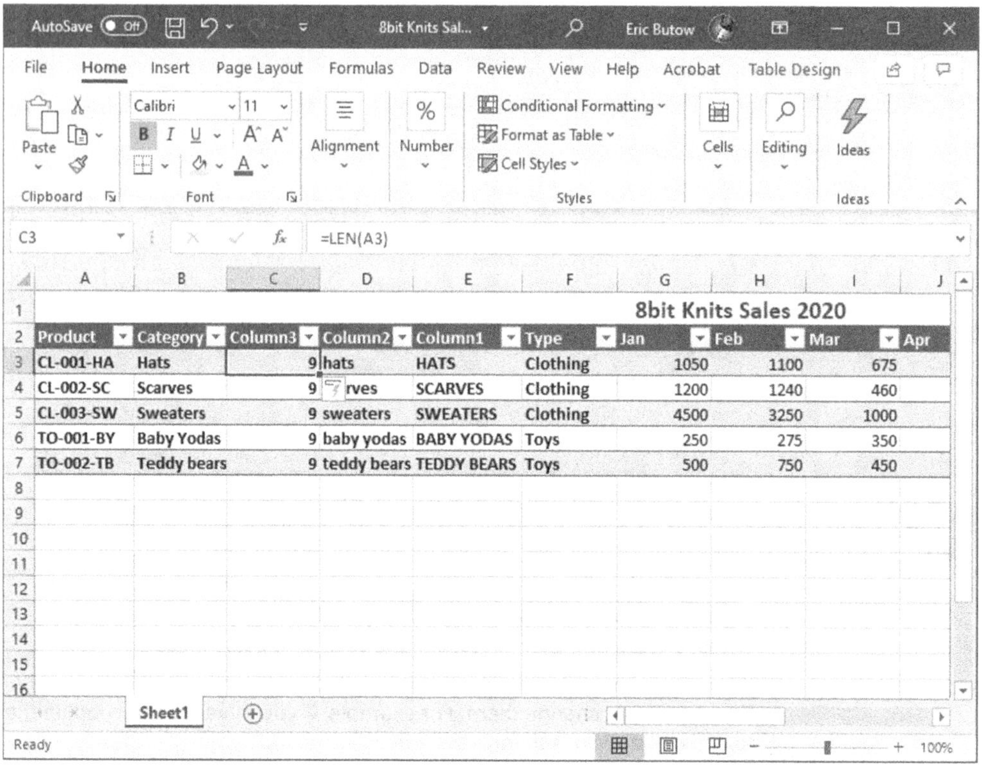

As with some other functions described in this chapter, Excel does not support the LEN() function in all languages, so if this function does not work, contact Microsoft to determine whether Excel supports this function for your language.

Formatting Text Using the *CONCAT()* and *TEXTJOIN()* Functions

When you need to join text from two or more cells and place the joined text into a new cell, Excel gives you two functions to do just that:

- CONCAT(), which replaces the CONCATENATE() function in earlier versions
- TEXTJOIN(), which is new in Excel 2019 and Excel for Microsoft Office 365

The Difference Between *CONCAT* and *TEXTJOIN*

Both the CONCAT() and TEXTJOIN() functions allow you to combine text. So, what's the difference?

- CONCAT() combines all text in two or more cells together with a delimiter such as a blank space. You simply add the range of cells you want to put together, and Excel shows you the combined text without any spaces in between.
- TEXTJOIN() gives you the option of adding a delimiter between each text string that you combine.

CONCAT()

Adding the CONCAT() function in the Formula Bar doesn't have as many arguments you need to add compared to TEXTJOIN(), but you don't get any options. Follow the steps in this example to see what I mean:

1. Click cell B9.
2. Type =CONCAT(B3:B4) in the Formula Bar.
3. Press Enter.

    You see the combined text from cells B3 and B4 in cell B9, as shown in Figure 4.22.

FIGURE 4.22 Combined text with CONCAT() function in the Formula Bar

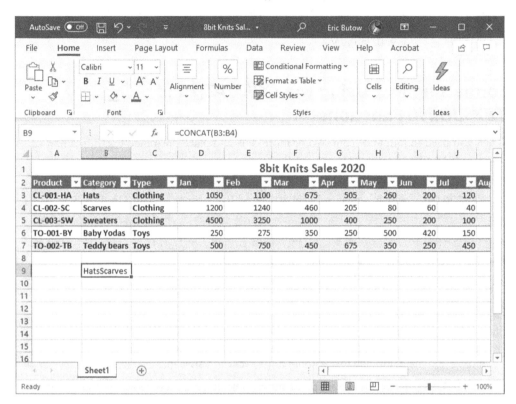

TEXTJOIN()

When you need to add spaces or another delimiter, such as a comma, between all the words in your combined text, the new TEXTJOIN() function is what you need. Here's how to use TEXTJOIN():

1. Click cell B10.

2. Type **=TEXTJOIN(" ",TRUE,B3:C5)** in the Formula Bar. The space between the quotes is a space, and the TRUE argument tells Excel to ignore any empty cells in the range.

3. Press Enter.

The combined text in the cell range appears in cell B10 (see Figure 4.23) with a space between each word.

FIGURE 4.23   The combined text with spaces between each text string

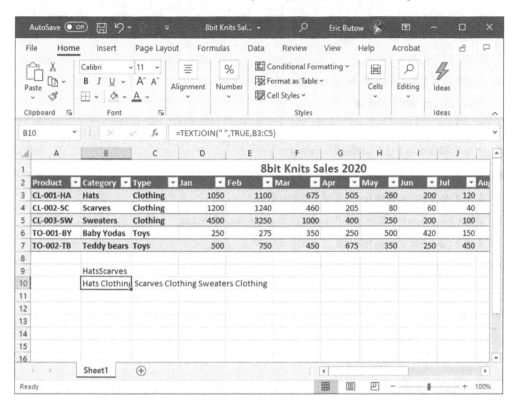

When you work with both the CONCAT() and TEXTJOIN() functions, keep the following in mind:

- You can type a text string within the formula instead of a cell reference, such as **=TEXTJOIN (" ",TRUE,"Microsoft","Excel")** or **=CONCAT("Micro","soft")** in the Formula Bar.

- With both the CONCAT() and TEXTJOIN() functions, the combined text string can be no longer than 32,767 characters. If the combined string is over that limit, then the cell with the CONCAT() or the TEXTJOIN() formula displays a #VALUE! error.

EXERCISE 4.3

Formatting and Modifying Text

1. Open a new document.

2. Add a new table with three columns and three rows.

3. Populate the table with text.

4. In cell A5, show the last five characters in cell A1.

5. In cell A6, show the first five characters in cell A2.

6. In cell A7, count five characters in the middle of the text starting with the third character.

7. Add a new column to the left of column B.

8. In the new column B, make the text in column A uppercase.

9. Add a new column to the left of column D.

10. In the new column D, make the text in column C lowercase.

11. In cell D5, get the length of cell D2.

12. In cell D6, join the text of cells D1 and D3 with a space delimiter.

Summary

This chapter started by showing you how to insert references in a worksheet or table, including relative, absolute, and mixed references. You also learned how to refer to named ranges and tables within a formula.

After you learned about references, you saw how to perform various calculations using built-in Excel functions, including the average, maximum, minimum, and sum functions. Then you learned how to count within cells using the three different counting functions in a formula. You also saw how to add the IF() function to perform conditional operations.

Next, I discussed how to format and modify text by using built-in functions to extract text from the right, left, and middle portions of a text string. You saw how to use functions to change text to all uppercase or all lowercase, as well as get the length of characters in a cell. Finally, you learned how to combine text in two or more cells together using the CONCAT() and TEXTJOIN() functions.

Key Terms

absolute

average

Formula Bar

maximum

minimum

mixed

references

relative

sum

Exam Essentials

Understand how to add relative, absolute, and mixed references in a formula. Know the correct terminology for adding a cell to a formula that will give you relative and absolute results. You must also know how to refer to a named range or table in a worksheet.

Know how to calculate numbers in one or more cells. Understand how to find the average, maximum, and minimum values in a range of cells that contain numbers. You also need to know how to sum a group of selected cells that have numbers.

Understand how to count cells. Know how to count the cells in a selected range that have numbers, how many cells are not empty, and how many cells are empty.

Know how to perform conditional operations. Understand how to determine if a condition is true or false.

Understand how to extract text from another cell. Know how to use built-in functions to extract from the right, left, or middle of a string of text in one cell and place the extracted text in another cell.

Be able to change the case of text and find the length of text in a cell. Know how to change one or more cells to all uppercase letters or all lowercase letters. You also need to understand how to find the length of a text string in one cell and display the length in another cell.

Know how to join text in two or more cells. Understand how to use the CONCAT() and TEXTJOIN() functions to join text in two or more cells and know the difference between each function.

Review Questions

1. In a formula, how do you change the reference quickly?

   A. Change the cell reference manually.

   B. Click the Format icon in the Home ribbon, and then click Format Cells.

   C. Press F4.

   D. Right-click in the Formula Bar, and then click Format Cells.

2. What counting function do you use to view all cells in a selected range that have text?

   A. COUNT()

   B. COUNTA()

   C. COUNTALL()

   D. COUNTBLANK()

3. What does the function =RIGHT(A3,5) do?

   A. It shows the first five characters in cell A3.

   B. It shows the five rows to the right of cell A3.

   C. It shows the last five characters in cell A3.

   D. It shows the first three characters and last five characters of all cells with text in column A.

4. What are the three reference types? (Choose all that apply.)

   A. Mixed

   B. Name

   C. Relative

   D. Absolute

5. What happens when you try to calculate the average of a range of cells when one or more cells does not have a number in it?

   A. The function treats the empty cell as the number *0*.

   B. The result of the function is an error message.

   C. The function returns the number *0*.

   D. The function ignores the empty cells.

6. What happens when you show the first five characters of a text string that includes a space?

   A. Excel ignores the space.

   B. Excel shows a dialog box with an error message.

   C. An error message appears in the cell.

   D. Excel shows the space.

7. A2 is what type of cell reference in a formula?
    A. Absolute
    B. Relative
    C. None
    D. Mixed

8. What do you type first in a formula?
    A. The formula name
    B. The left parenthesis
    C. The equal sign
    D. A colon

9. What function do you use when you want to combine text in two cells and not have a space between the combined text?
    A. CONCAT()
    B. TEXTJOIN()
    C. SUM()
    D. COUNT()

10. What do you do when you want to summarize cells in multiple ranges?
    A. Type each SUM() formula for each range separated by a comma.
    B. Add all of the cells individually within the parentheses in the SUM() formula.
    C. Type each SUM() formula for each range separated by a plus (+) sign.
    D. Add a comma between each cell range within the parentheses in the formula.

Chapter

5

Managing Charts

MICROSOFT EXAM OBJECTIVES COVERED IN THIS CHAPTER:

✓ **Manage charts**

- Create charts
  - Create charts
  - Create chart sheets
- Modify charts
  - Add data series to charts
  - Switch between rows and columns in source data
  - Add and modify chart elements
- Format charts
  - Apply chart layouts
  - Apply chart styles
  - Add alternative text to charts for accessibility

A chart is an effective way to grasp data in a worksheet visually. You may remember how you had to create charts in math classes in school, where you learned the relationship between data and a graph. It should come as no surprise that Excel has charts built in since Excel deals a lot with math.

I start by showing you how to create charts, both in the same worksheet and in a separate worksheet in a workbook. Next, you'll learn how to modify charts by adding data series, switching between rows and columns, as well as adding and modifying various chart elements.

Finally, you'll learn how to format a chart by adding layouts, styles, and Alt text (short for alternative text) to a chart, which helps you better explain what a chart is about.

Creating Charts

If you used an older version of Excel before version 2019, or the version for Microsoft Office 365, you may have used Chart Wizard to create a chart. In that case, you will be disappointed to learn that the Chart Wizard is not included in the latest versions of Excel.

Even so, Microsoft still makes it easy to create charts in the latest versions of Excel. You can build a chart, both within an existing worksheet and as a separate worksheet within your workbook, so that it's easier for readers to move back and forth quickly between a worksheet with data and a worksheet with a chart, which references that data.

Building Charts

So, how do you build a chart? After you open a workbook that contains a worksheet with numerical data, here's how to find the chart you want and add it to your worksheet:

1. Select the cells you want to use to create a chart.
2. Click the Insert menu option.
3. In the Charts section in the Insert ribbon, click the Recommended Charts icon, as shown in Figure 5.1.

FIGURE 5.1 The Recommended Charts icon in the Insert ribbon

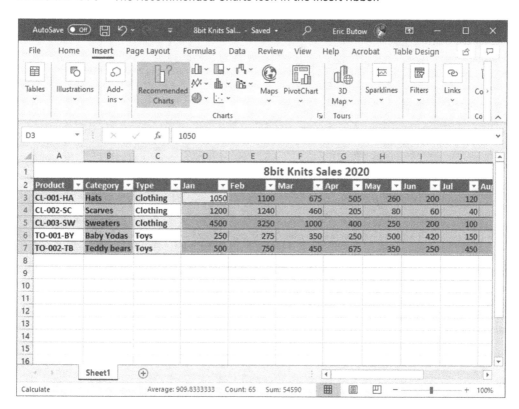

4. In the Insert Chart dialog box that appears in Figure 5.2, scroll up and down the list of recommended charts in the Recommended Charts tab. Click a chart type in the list to view a sample of how the chart will look as well as a description of what the chart is about and when to use it.

5. Select the All Charts tab to view a list of all charts. The Column category is selected in the list on the left side of the dialog box (see Figure 5.3).

   The column chart area appears at the right side of the dialog box; the column type icon is selected at the top of the area.

6. Move the mouse pointer over the column type to view a larger preview of the chart.

7. For this example, select the Recommended tab and add the Clustered Column chart that you saw in Figure 5.2.

8. Click OK.

   The chart appears below the table in the example, as shown in Figure 5.4.

FIGURE 5.2   The Insert Chart dialog box

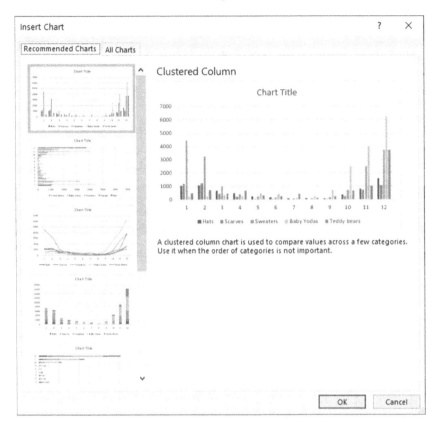

Now your text is in the table, though you may have to do some more tweaking to get it to appear the way you want it to look.

You can resize the chart by clicking and holding one of the circular sizing handles and then dragging the chart in the direction that you want. If you want to resize both the horizontal and vertical size of the chart, click and drag one of the corner sizing handles.

Working with Chart Sheets

When you don't want to have a chart appear with the same worksheet, Excel makes it easy to create a new chart in a new worksheet. Microsoft calls this a *chart sheet*, and you may find it most useful if you are creating a chart from a large amount of data.

For example, instead of having your viewers scroll around your worksheet to find the chart, you can make it easy for them to view the chart with one click of the worksheet tab that contains your chart sheet.

FIGURE 5.3   The Column category in the All Charts tab

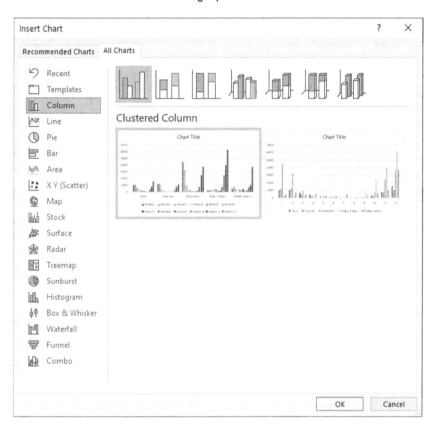

Create a chart sheet by following these steps:

1. Create a chart as you learned to do earlier in this chapter. I will use the chart I created earlier in this chapter for this example.
2. Click anywhere in the chart.
3. Click the Chart Design menu option.
4. In the Location section in the Chart Design ribbon, click the Move Chart icon, as shown in Figure 5.5.
5. In the Move Chart dialog box (see Figure 5.6), click the New Sheet radio button.
6. Type a new name if you want by pressing the Backspace key and then typing the new name in the New Sheet text box. For this example, leave the default Chart1 name.
7. Click OK.

FIGURE 5.4   The chart in the worksheet

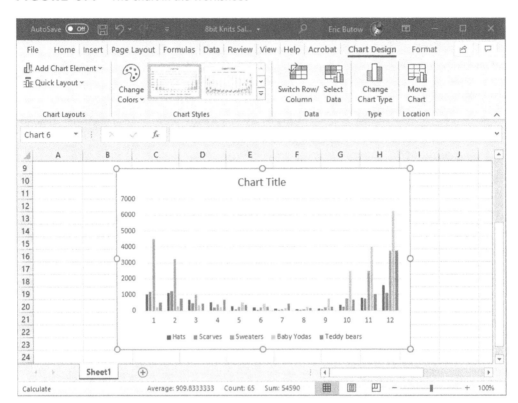

A new worksheet appears, as shown in Figure 5.7, and the chart takes up the entirety of the worksheet space.

The chart sheet tab appears to the left of the worksheet tab. Click the worksheet tab to view the worksheet data without the chart.

Though there are sizing handles that bound the chart in the chart sheet, you cannot resize the chart using those sizing handles.

EXERCISE 5.1

Creating Charts

1.   Open a new workbook.

2.   In the worksheet, add a header row with text in four columns.

3. Add numbers into four rows within all the columns.

4. Create a Clustered Column chart for the entire table.

5. Move the chart to a new chart sheet.

6. Save the workbook.

FIGURE 5.5 Move Chart icon in the Chart Design ribbon

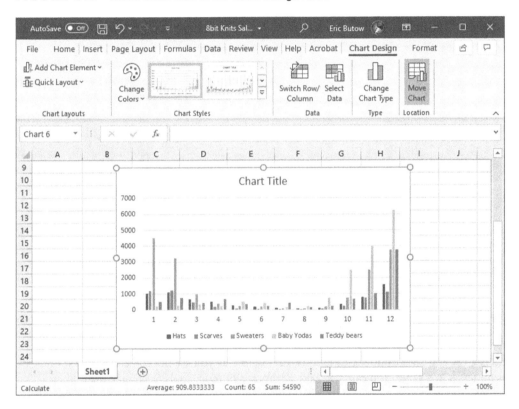

FIGURE 5.6 Move Chart dialog box

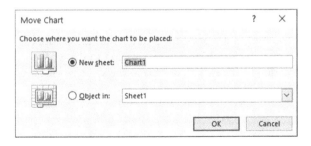

FIGURE 5.7   The chart in a new tab

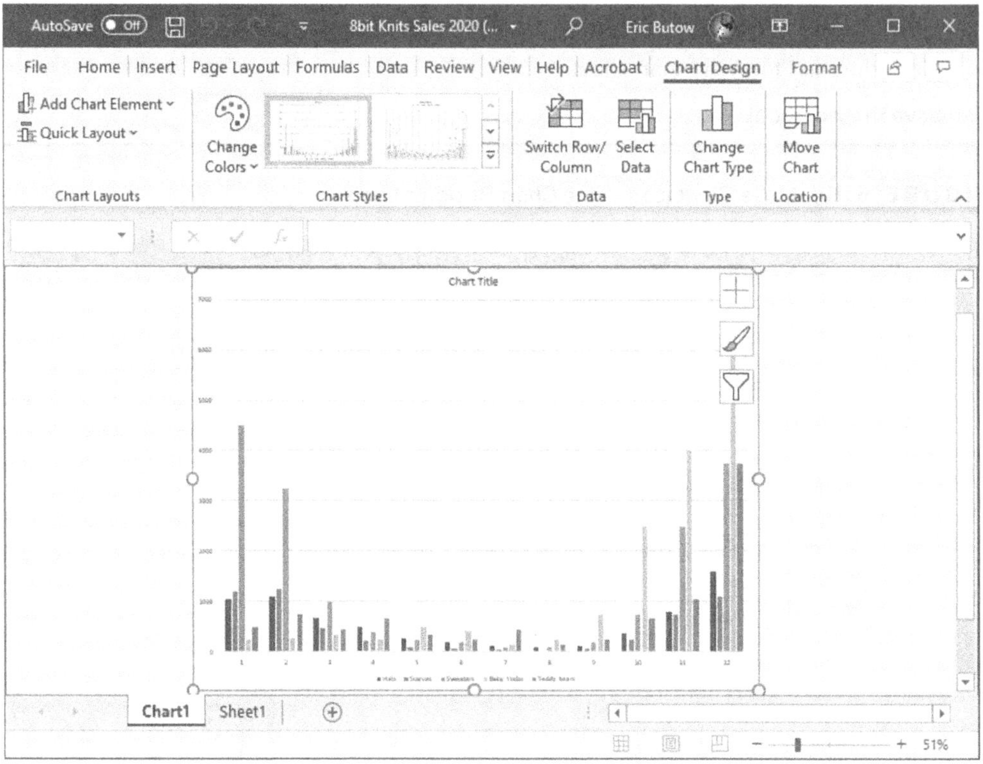

Modifying Charts

Excel gives you a lot of power to modify your charts as you see fit. You can sort text and/or numbers in a table. You can also take advantage of more tools to change the look of the text and graphics in your chart, align your chart in the worksheet, and even change the chart type.

Adding Data Series to Charts

A *data series* is one or more rows and/or columns in a worksheet or table that Excel uses to build a chart. After you add a chart, you may want to add more information to the worksheet and have Excel update the chart accordingly. It's easy to do this in the same worksheet chart and in a chart sheet.

Add a Data Series in the Same Worksheet Chart

Follow these steps to add a data series to a chart in the same worksheet:

1. Click the chart if necessary. The corresponding rows and/or columns of data appear in the worksheet or table.

2. In the worksheet or table, click and hold the sizing handle at the bottom right of the selection that you want to add.

3. Drag the sizing handle to place the selection over the data you want to include.

4. Release the mouse button.

The selection box in the worksheet or table now reflects your changes, and the chart shows new bars that reflect the data in column F (see Figure 5.8).

FIGURE 5.8   The updated chart and expanded selection area in the table

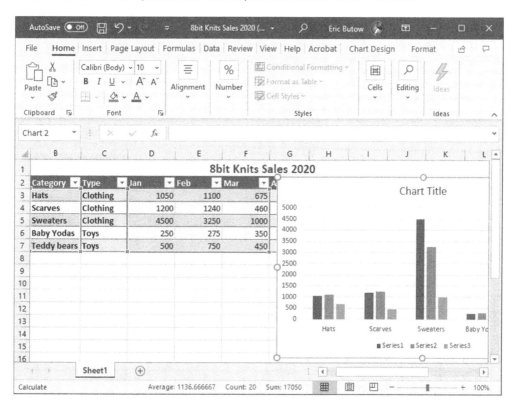

Add a Data Series to a Chart Sheet

When you have a chart sheet based on data in another worksheet, and you have a lot of data in that worksheet, then selecting a large range may not be a practical option. In this case, Excel allows you to add a data series within the chart sheet. Here's how to do it:

1. At the bottom of the Excel window, click the sheet tab that contains the chart. In this example, the chart sheet name is Chart1.

2. In the Data section in the Chart Design menu ribbon, click Select Data.

3. The Select Data Source dialog box opens, and the worksheet with your data appears in the Excel window (see Figure 5.9).

FIGURE 5.9   Select Data Source dialog box and selected table cells

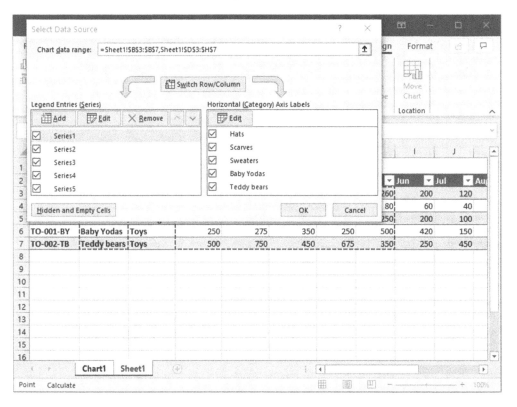

4. Press and hold the Ctrl key as you click and drag on more cells that you want to add to the chart.

5. When you select all the cells in the worksheet or table, release the Ctrl key and the mouse button.

6. Click OK in the Select Data Source dialog box.

In this example, the updated chart with the added bars for the month of June appears in the chart sheet (see Figure 5.10).

FIGURE 5.10   Updated chart in chart sheet

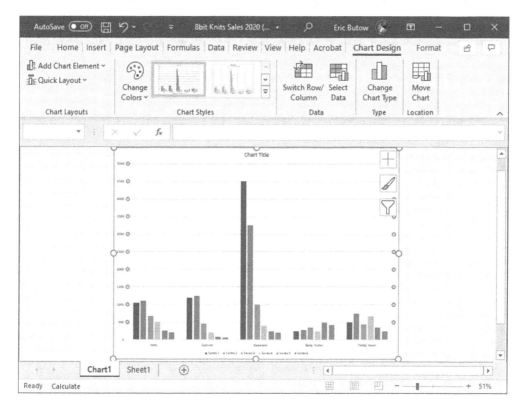

Switching Between Rows and Columns in Source Data

Excel follows one rule when it creates a chart: the larger number of rows or columns is placed in the horizontal axis. For example, if there are 12 columns and 5 rows, then columns are along the horizontal axis.

But what if you want the rows to appear in the horizontal axis? Excel makes it easy. Start by clicking the chart in your worksheet or in the chart sheet. In the Data section in the Chart Design menu ribbon, click Switch Row/Column.

Now the axes have switched, as you can see in Figure 5.11, so you can determine whether you like it. If you don't, click Switch Row/Column in the Chart Design ribbon again.

What happens if you have equal numbers of rows and columns in your worksheet or table? Excel uses the same layout as rows and columns in a worksheet: columns for the horizontal axis and rows for the vertical axis.

FIGURE 5.11 Row titles in the horizontal axis

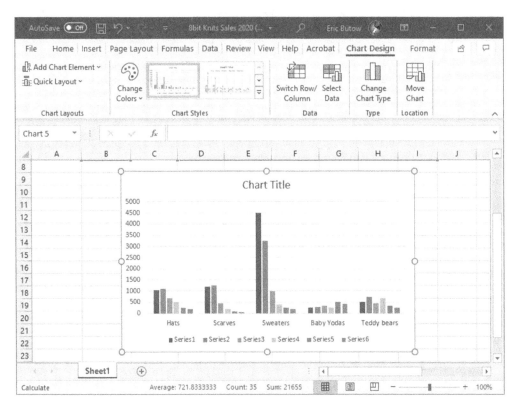

Adding and Modifying Chart Elements

It's easy to add and modify the elements you see in a chart. You can view a list of elements that you can add to the chart by clicking anywhere in the chart and then clicking the Chart Elements icon at the upper-right corner of the chart.

A list of the elements appears, with check boxes to the left of each element name, as shown in Figure 5.12.

Selected check boxes indicate that the element is currently applied. Cleared check boxes mean that the element is not applied. When you move the mouse pointer over the element in the list, you see how the element will appear in the chart—that is, if the element is not already applied.

The following is a list of the elements you can add and remove from your chart:

Axes These are the horizonal and vertical units of measure in the chart. In the sample chart shown in Figure 5.12, the horizontal units represent products sold and the vertical units represent sales in increments of 1,000. Excel shows the axes by default.

FIGURE 5.12   Chart elements list

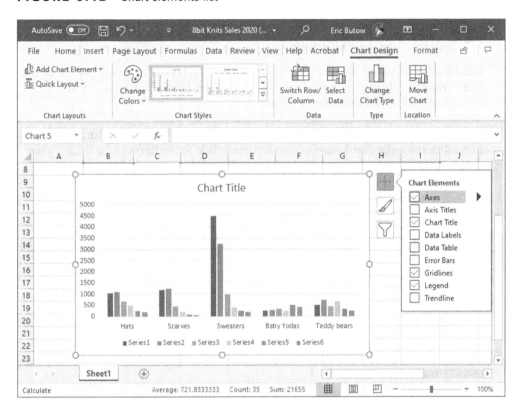

Axis Titles   These are the titles for the vertical and horizontal axes. The default name of each title is Axis Title. You can change the title after you add it by double-clicking within the title, selecting the text, and then typing your own text.

Chart Title   Excel automatically shows the title of your chart, which is Chart Title by default. You can change this title by double-clicking Chart Title, selecting the text, and then typing a new title.

Data Labels   These add the number in each cell above each corresponding point or bar in the chart. If your points or bars are close together, having data labels can be difficult to read because the numbers can overlap.

Data Table   This places your selected cells in a table below the chart. If you have a large table, then you may need to enlarge the size of the chart in the worksheet.

Error Bars   If you have a chart with data that has margins of error, such as political polls, you can add *error bars* to your chart to show those margins. Error bars also work when you want to see the standard deviation, which measures how widely a range of values are from the mean.

Gridlines   This displays the gridlines behind the lines or bars in a graph. Gridlines are active by default.

Legend   Excel shows the *legend*, which explains what each line or bar color represents, at the bottom of the chart by default.

Trendline   A *trendline* is a straight or curved line that shows the overall pattern of the data in the chart. In the example shown in Figure 5.13, I can check to see the trendline for sales of teddy bears throughout the year.

Once I select the Trendlines check box, the Add Trendline dialog box appears and asks me to click the series that I want to check. After I click Teddy Bears in the list and then click OK, the dashed line appears and the trendline also appears in the legend (see Figure 5.13).

FIGURE 5.13   Trend line for teddy bears

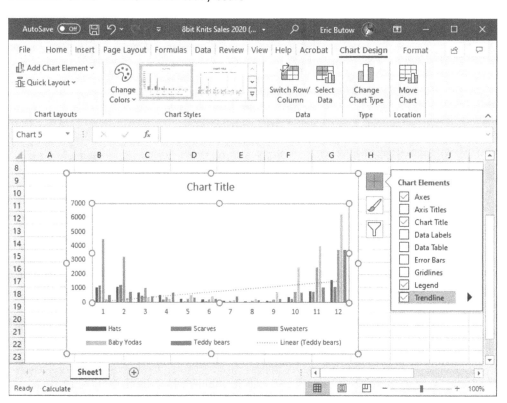

Change Elements More Precisely

An arrow appears to the right of each element name. When you click the arrow, a secondary menu with more precise options, as well as an option for viewing even more options, appears. For example, you can hide the vertical axis label but keep the horizontal axis label.

When you click More Options in the secondary menu, the Format panel appears at the right side of the Excel window so that you can make even more specific changes, such as making the chart title text outlined instead of solid.

EXERCISE 5.2

Modifying Charts

1.   Open the workbook that you created in Exercise 5.1 if it's not already open.

2.   Add a new column to the worksheet.

3.   Populate the column with text in the first row and numbers in the remaining rows.

4.   Add the new column to the chart.

5.   Reverse the axes.

6.   Add a trendline.

Formatting Charts

When you need to format your chart, click within the chart to view the two formatting ribbons:

- Click the Chart Design menu option to add and change chart styles. The Chart Design ribbon appears after you create your chart.
- Click the Format menu option to change formats of the various elements in your ribbon.

When you click in an area outside of your chart and then click the chart again, Excel remembers the menu ribbon that you last used and opens that ribbon automatically.

Microsoft has identified three common tasks when you create a chart, and so those tasks are in the MO-200 exam: apply a chart layout, apply chart styles, and add alternative text, which is also known by the shorthand term *Alt text*.

Using Chart Layouts

After you create a chart, Excel applies its default layout to the chart. Microsoft realizes that you may not want this layout, but you also may not want to take the time to create your own custom layout. So, Excel contains not only the default layout but also 10 other built-in layouts that you can apply to a chart. Follow these steps to apply a chart layout:

1. Click the chart if necessary. The corresponding rows and/or columns of data appear in the worksheet or table.

2. Click the Chart Design menu option if necessary.

3. In the Chart Layouts section in the Chart Design ribbon, click the Quick Layout icon.

4. Move the mouse pointer over the layout tile in the drop-down menu. As you move the mouse pointer over each layout, the chart style in your worksheet or chart sheet changes so that you can see how the style looks (see Figure 5.14).

FIGURE 5.14   Excel previews the layout in the chart.

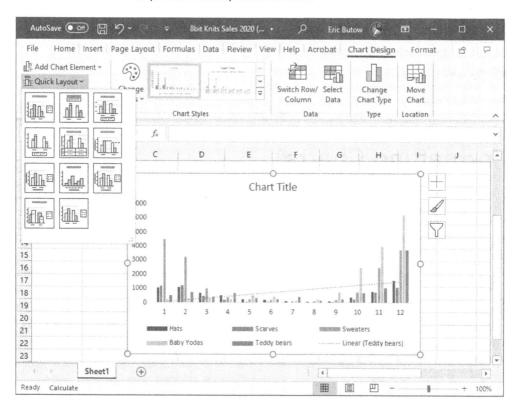

5. When you find a chart layout, click the tile in the drop-down menu.

Excel applies the chart layout that you previewed into the chart.

Create Your Own Chart Layout

You may like some parts of the built-in layout that you selected but not others. Excel gives you the ability to change different parts of your chart layout to suit your needs.

Start by clicking the chart and then clicking the Format menu option if necessary. In the Format ribbon, which is shown in Figure 5.15, you can select options within the following seven ribbon sections.

FIGURE 5.15 Format ribbon sections

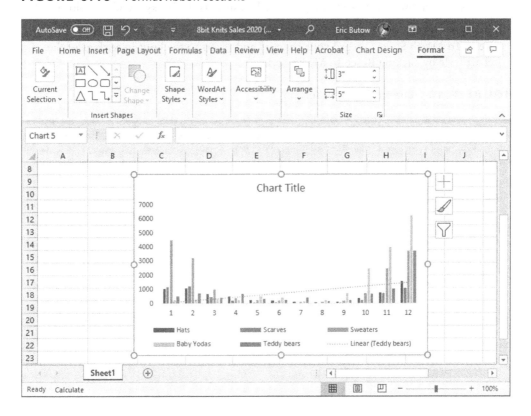

As you work with the Format ribbon, keep the following in mind:

- In the screenshots shown in this chapter, the width of the Excel window is 800 pixels. If your window is wider, however, then you will see most or all of the options in each section without having to click the section name.

- Different parts of the ribbon will be disabled depending on the portion of the chart that you want to edit. For example, when you click the chart title, the width and height setting options in the Size section are disabled.

- The Format ribbon changes when you perform certain actions. For example, when you add a shape, the Shape Format ribbon replaces the Format ribbon so that you can edit the shape. Shape formatting options are beyond the purview of this book.

Current Selection

In the Current Selection section on the left side of the ribbon (see Figure 5.16), you can change the following settings:

Chart Area: The current area that you're editing appears in the area box. Click the down arrow to the right of the box to view a drop-down list of all the areas that you can edit. Select an area to edit by clicking the area in the list.

Format Selection: Click Format Selection to open the Format pane on the right side of the Excel window and make more precise edits, such as the background fill color for the horizontal axis.

Reset To Match Style: Discard your changes and revert to the built-in settings of the chart style by clicking Reset To Match Style.

FIGURE 5.16   Current Selection section

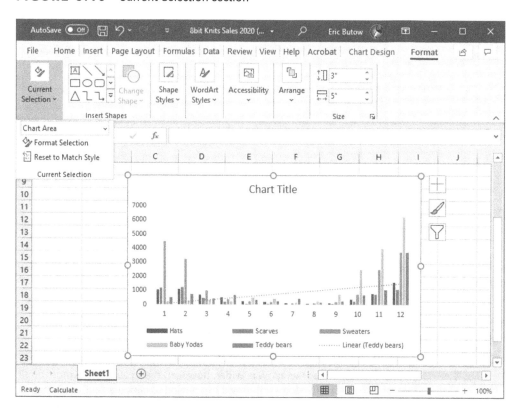

Insert Shapes

In the Insert Shapes section, shown in Figure 5.17, you can insert shapes as separate elements in the chart by clicking the shape icon.

FIGURE 5.17   Insert Shapes section

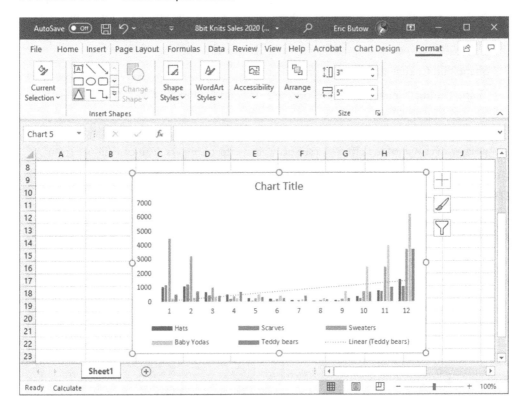

If you don't see the shape you want, click the More button to the right of the icons. (The More button looks like a down arrow with a line above it.) Then you can select the shape icon from the drop-down list.

Add the shape by following these steps:

1. Move the mouse pointer where you want to add the shape.
2. Click and hold down the mouse button.
3. Drag the mouse pointer until the shape is the size you want.
4. Release the mouse button.

Once you add a shape, you can make changes to your shape in the Shape Format ribbon.

Shape Styles

The Shape Styles area, shown in Figure 5.18, allows you to apply the following features to a shape:

Shape Styles: Click one of the seven shape style icons to change the shape border color. If you don't like any of those style colors, click the More button to the right of the icon row. (The More button looks like a down arrow with a line above it.) From the drop-down list that appears, you can select a style with your desired border, text, and/or fill colors.

Shape Fill: Change the fill color or background.

Shape Outline: Change the shape border color and thickness as well as the outline to a solid or dashed line.

Shape Effects: Add an effect to a shape. In the drop-down menu, move the mouse pointer over one of the effects to see how each effect appears. You can choose from Preset, Shadow, Reflection, Glow, Bevel, 3-D Rotation, or Transform.

FIGURE 5.18   Shape Styles section

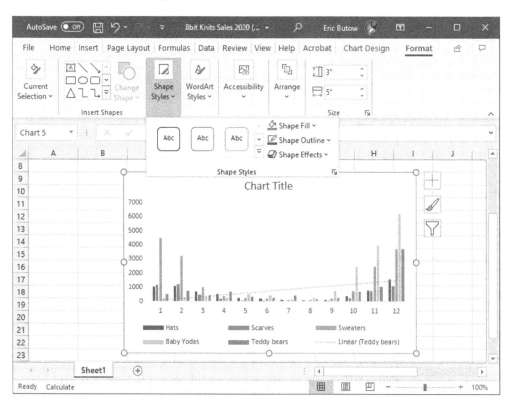

WordArt Styles

WordArt is Microsoft's term for special effects applied to text in Word, Outlook, Power-Point, and Excel. In the WordArt Styles section, click one of the three built-in text effect icons (see Figure 5.19).

FIGURE 5.19   WordArt Styles section

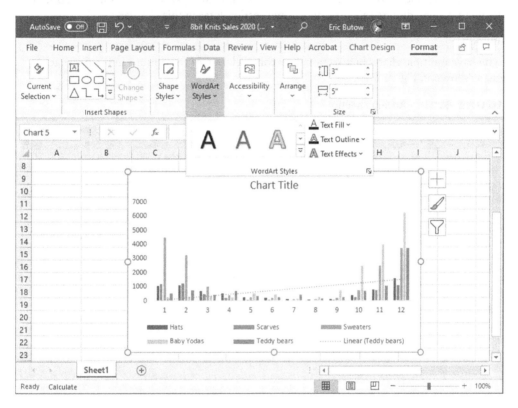

You can view more styles by clicking the More button to the right of the text effect icon row. (The More button looks like a down arrow with a line above it.) Then you can select the style from the drop-down list.

If you want to create your own style, click one of the following icons:

Text Fill: Change the text color in the drop-down menu.

Text Outline: Add an outline, including color and outline line width, using the drop-down menu.

Text Effects: View and add other effects to the text. In the drop-down menu, move the mouse pointer over one of the effects to see how the effect appears in your photo. You can choose from Preset, Shadow, Reflection, Glow, Bevel, 3-D Rotation, and Transform.

Accessibility

Click the Alt Text icon to add alternative text to your chart. This information is important enough that I will discuss this topic in its own section later in this chapter.

Arrange

If you have multiple charts in a section, you can click one of the options in the Arrange section, as shown in Figure 5.20.

FIGURE 5.20   Arrange section

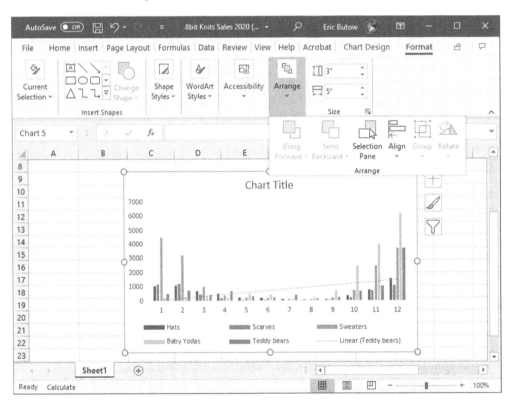

For example, click Selection Pane to open the Selection panel on the right side of the Excel window so that you can see all the charts, and choose to hide a chart for some reviewers who don't need to see it but show the chart again if you want to display the chart for other reviewers.

Size

Change the exact height and width by clicking the Height and the Width box, respectively (see Figure 5.21).

FIGURE 5.21 Size section

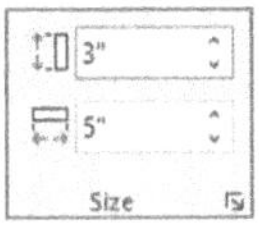

You can type the height and width in inches as precise as hundredths of an inch. To the right of the Height and Width boxes, click the up and down arrows to increase or decrease the height by one tenth of an inch.

 When you select the entire chart and then make changes, all of those changes are made within that chart. However, if you make changes to one area of the chart, such as the vertical axis, then the changes apply only to the one area that you edited.

Align Multiple Charts in a Worksheet

You have two charts in a worksheet that you're going to share with the executives in your company. Although you want to make the charts easy to read, you don't want to take the time to move each chart and get them aligned in the way you want.

You can take advantage of the alignment features in Excel to align multiple charts as follows:

1. Select both charts by holding down the Shift key and then selecting each chart.

2. Click the Shape Format menu option.

3. In the Arrange section in the Shape Format ribbon, click Align.

Now you can align the charts vertically (left, center, and right) or horizontally (top, middle, or bottom). If both charts have similar horizontal and/or vertical positions, as shown in the screenshot here, then your alignment may result in one chart overlapping the other.

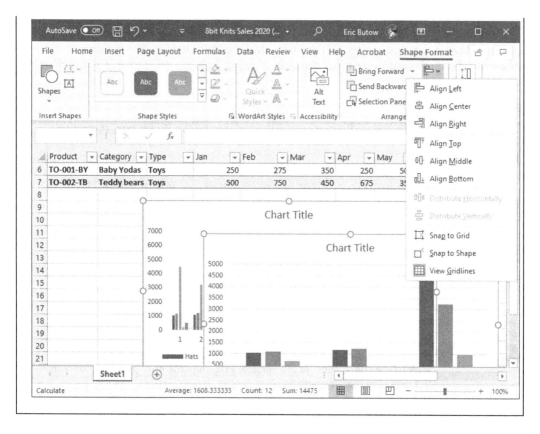

Applying Chart Styles

When you create a chart, Excel applies its default style for the type of chart you select in the Insert Chart dialog box that you learned about earlier in this chapter. If you don't like that style, you can add one of an additional 13 styles.

Excel also allows you to make changes to a style to make the chart look the way you want. Before you can make changes to a style, you must apply the built-in style.

Apply a Built-In Chart Style

Here's how to apply one of the built-in styles to your chart:

1. Click the chart if necessary. The corresponding rows and/or columns of data appear in the worksheet or table.

2. Click the Chart Design menu option if necessary.

3. In the Chart Styles section in the Chart Design ribbon, click the More button to the right of the last chart style tile in the row. (The More button looks like a down arrow with a line above it.)

4. Move the mouse pointer over the style tile in the drop-down menu. As you move the mouse pointer over each style, the chart style in your worksheet or chart sheet changes so that you can see how the style looks (see Figure 5.22).

FIGURE 5.22 The preview of the style in the chart

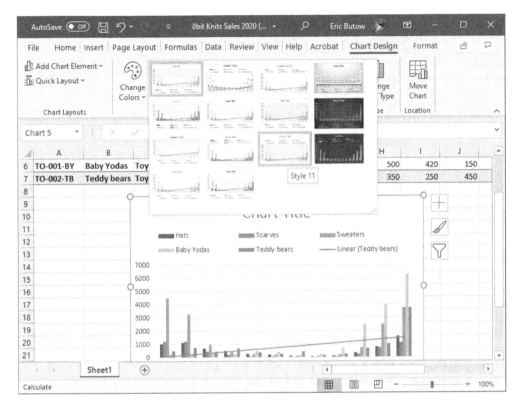

5. When you find a chart style, click the tile in the drop-down menu.

Excel applies the chart style that you previewed into the chart.

Create Your Own Chart Style

After you apply a chart style, you can modify it in only one way: the color scheme. To do that, follow these steps:

1. Click the chart if necessary. The corresponding rows and/or columns of data appear in the worksheet or table.

2. Click the Chart Design menu option if necessary.

3. In the Chart Styles section in the Chart Design ribbon, click the Change Colors icon.

4. Swipe up and down in the list of color swatch groups. There are six colors in each swatch group (see Figure 5.23).

FIGURE 5.23   Six swatch colors in the selected swatch group

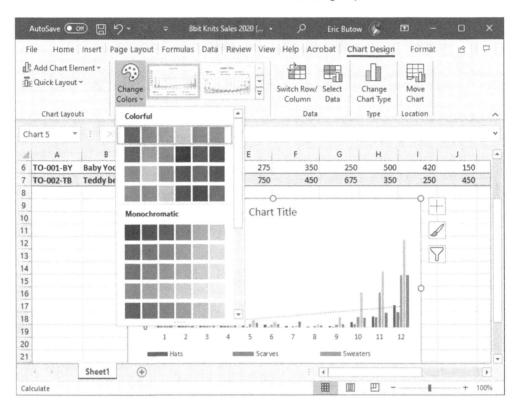

5. As you move the mouse pointer over each swatch group, the colors in the chart change so that you can see how they look. When you find a color swatch you like, click the swatch group in the list.

    Excel applies the color swatch group to all elements in the chart.

> You can edit specific colors in a chart, such as bars for one series of data, by clicking the color in the chart and then clicking the Format menu option. Then you can change the color as you learned to do earlier in this chapter.

Adding Alternative Text to Charts for Accessibility

Alt text, or alternative text, tells anyone who views your document in Excel what the chart is when the reader moves their mouse pointer over it. If the reader can't see your document, then Excel will use text-to-speech in Windows to read your Alt text to the reader audibly.

Here's how to add Alt text:

1. Click the chart if necessary.

2. Click the Format menu option if necessary.

3. In the Accessibility section in the Format ribbon, click the Alt Text icon. (If your Excel window isn't very wide, you may need to click the Accessibility icon and then click Alt Text.)

4. In the Alt Text pane on the right side of the Excel window (see Figure 5.24), type one or two sentences in the text box to describe the object and its context.

FIGURE 5.24   Alt Text pane

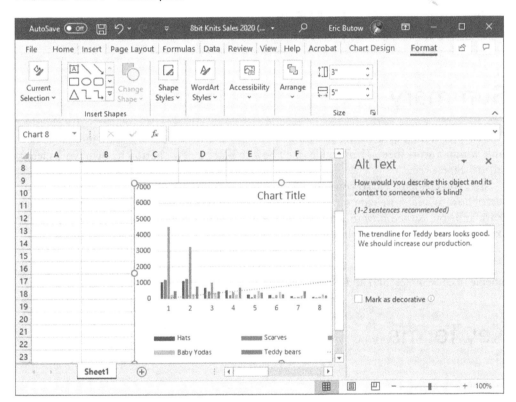

5. Click the Mark As Decorative check box if your chart adds visual interest but doesn't require a description.

6. When you're done, close the pane.

EXERCISE 5.3

Formatting Charts

1.   Open a workbook that contains numerical data.

2.   Create a chart in the worksheet, if necessary.

3.   Change the chart style to another one of your choice.

4.   Add a new shape of your choice into the chart.

5.   Change the shape style to another one of your choice.

6.   Apply a new color scheme to your chart.

7.   Add Alt text that describes your chart.

Summary

This chapter started by showing you how to create a chart from selected data in a range or table within a worksheet. Then you learned how to place a new chart in its own worksheet, called a chart sheet.

After you created a chart, you learned how to modify the chart to suit your needs. I discussed how to add more data series to a chart. Next, you learned how to switch the axes in a chart, and you learned how to modify the look and feel of your chart, including the axes, the axis and chart titles, data labels, the data table, error bars, gridlines, the legend, and trendlines.

Finally, you learned how to use and apply chart layouts, apply and change the color scheme in chart styles, and add alternative text to a chart.

Key Terms

Alt text	error bars
chart	legend
chart sheet	trendline
data series	WordArt

Exam Essentials

Understand how to create a chart.   Know how to create a chart by accessing the Insert Chart dialog box and then selecting either a recommended chart or one of the many chart types Excel has available.

Know how to create a chart sheet.   Understand how to create a chart that appears separately within an entire worksheet.

Understand how to add a data series to a chart.   Know how to add additional cells in a worksheet or a table into a chart after you have already created the chart.

Know how to switch between row and column data in a chart.   Understand how Excel places data series in the horizontal and vertical axes as well as how to switch those axes in a chart.

Understand how to add and modify chart elements.   Know how to add chart elements to your chart—including axes, axis titles, the chart title, data labels in the chart, a data table in the chart, error bars, gridlines, a legend, and a trendline—and be able to modify those elements.

Be able to apply chart layouts.   Know how to apply a different chart layout using the Quick Layout menu in the Chart Design ribbon.

Know how to select and change chart styles.   Know how to apply a chart style from the Chart Design ribbon as well as change the color scheme for the style.

Understand how to add Alt text.   Know why Alt text is important for your readers and how to add Alt text to a chart.

Review Questions

1. How do you view a list of all charts that you can create?

   A. Click the Change Chart Type icon in the Chart Design ribbon.

   B. Click a new style tile in the Chart Design ribbon.

   C. Select the All Charts tab in the Insert Chart dialog box.

   D. Click the Chart Elements icon in the upper-right corner of the selected chart.

2. If you create a chart from a worksheet or table that has equal numbers of columns and rows, what does Excel use as the horizontal axis?

   A. A dialog box appears and asks you if you want to use rows or columns.

   B. Columns

   C. Rows

   D. An error message appears in a dialog box.

3. What types of styles can be applied when you format a chart? (Choose all that apply.)

   A. Shapes

   B. Chart area

   C. WordArt

   D. Size

4. What do you need to add to a chart that explains what each line or bar color represents?

   A. Legend

   B. Data labels

   C. Data table

   D. Axis titles

5. What shape attributes can you change with a built-in style? (Choose all that apply.)

   A. Border color

   B. Text size

   C. Text color

   D. Background color

6. How do you change a data element in your chart more precisely?

   A. Click Add Chart Element in the Chart Design ribbon and then click the type of element that you want to edit.

   B. Click Format Selection in the Format ribbon.

   C. Click the right arrow next to the element name in the Chart Elements list.

   D. Click Quick Layout in the Chart Design ribbon and then select the appropriate layout from the drop-down menu.

7. How do you resize a chart in the chart sheet?

    A. Click and drag one of the sizing handles at the boundary of the chart.

    B. You can't resize it.

    C. Set the measurement in the Format ribbon.

    D. Resize the chart in the worksheet before you move the chart to its own chart sheet.

8. Why do you add a trendline in a bar chart?

    A. To better show the levels of a bar in a chart

    B. Because Excel requires it before you can save the chart

    C. To see the overall trend of data over time

    D. To show the margins of error in a chart

9. What is the difference between a chart layout and a chart style?

    A. They're the same thing.

    B. The chart layout lets you change the type of chart, and the chart style changes the look and feel of the chart.

    C. The chart layout applies the chart style elements to the chart.

    D. A chart layout shows chart elements, and chart styles change how the chart looks.

10. Why should you add Alt text to a chart?

    A. Because it's required for all charts in an Excel workbook

    B. To help people who can't see the chart know what the graphic is about

    C. Because Excel won't save your workbook until you do

    D. Because you want to be as informative as possible

Appendix

Answers to Review Questions

Chapter 1: Managing Worksheets and Workbooks

1. A, C. A text file uses a tab character as the delimiter, and a comma-separated value file uses a comma as the delimiter.

2. B. Type the tilde (~) before the question mark to ensure that Excel finds text in cells with a question mark.

3. C. When you double-click the right edge of the column within the header, such as to the right of the B column, Excel automatically adjusts the width to the text in a cell that has the greatest width.

4. B, D. You can only add tools and commands to the Quick Access Toolbar.

5. A, B, D. You can save to PDF format, text format, and HTML, which is the language used to create web pages.

6. A, D. The Quick Access Toolbar is in the title bar by default, but you can also move it under the ribbon.

7. B. When you add a Screen Tip, a pop-up box appears when you move the mouse pointer over the link.

8. C. You can add a header and/or footer from within Page Layout view.

9. C. You must protect the worksheet by clicking the Review menu option and then clicking Protect Sheet in the Protect section in the Review menu ribbon.

10. D. Click the Page Layout menu option to open the Page Layout ribbon. Next, click Print Area in the Page Setup section and then select Set Print Area from the drop-down menu.

Chapter 2: Using Data Cells and Ranges

1. B. When you select the Formulas And Number Formatting icon from the Paste drop-down menu, Excel copies only the formatting in the formulas and any number formatting into the new cell.

2. C. When you select Merge Across from the Merge & Center drop-down menu in the Home ribbon, the selected cells merge and the data in the first column within the selected cells is left-aligned.

3. B, D. You can only start a named range with letters and underscores.

4. D. When you click a blank cell and press Ctrl+A, Excel selects all cells in the worksheet.

5.   A. Place the Sparkline chart after the last column in a row to have the Sparkline collect its data from all columns within the row.

6.   A, B, D. You can Auto Fill sequential information, including numbers, dates, and months of the year. You can also Auto Fill a number in one cell into one or more other cells.

7.   C. When you select Format Cell Alignment from the menu, you can specify the angle in degrees.

8.   C. When you click Greater, you can format cells with numbers that are greater than a specific value in the Greater Than dialog box.

9.   C. A named range can be no longer than 255 characters, including spaces.

10. A, C, D. You can apply the Accounting Number style (the $ icon) for the type of currency, the Percent style (the % icon), and the Comma style for numbers larger than 999.

Chapter 3: Working with Tables and Table Data

1.   C. Excel applies the formatting from your table to the cell range.

2.   B, D. You can press Ctrl+Z to undo the deletion, or you can click the Undo icon in the Quick Access Toolbar if you prefer to use the mouse.

3.   C. Sorting from Z to A is descending order. Sorting from A to Z is ascending order.

4.   A, C, D. In the Format Cells dialog box, you can change the font, border, and fill color and pattern in the appropriate tabs.

5.   D. The Count Numbers option shows you the total number of cells in the column that have numbers in them.

6.   A, B, D. In the Table Design menu ribbon, the Header Row, Banded Rows, and Filter Button check boxes are checked by default.

7.   A, B. The header row and filter button are two features that appear automatically in your new table.

8.   C. You need to sort by column in a custom sort, and you can select the column you want to use for the sort.

9.   B. Excel totals the last (or rightmost) column in a table.

10. D. Several style tiles appear in the Table Styles section within the Table Design menu ribbon that opens after you create a table.

Chapter 4: Performing Operations by Using Formulas and Functions

1. C. As you press F4 on the keyboard, the cell reference type cycles between all three types.

2. B. The COUNTA() function counts all cells in a selected range that have characters in them and returns the number of cells Excel found.

3. C. The RIGHT() function shows the last five characters, or the five characters at the right, of the text in cell A3.

4. A, C, D. You can create a mixed, relative, or absolute cell reference type in a formula.

5. D. The function does not count empty cells when you average numbers within a range of cells.

6. D. The LEFT() function treats spaces as characters, so spaces appear in the cell where you entered the LEFT() formula.

7. B. Using A2 without any $ signs in the cell reference indicates that this is a relative cell reference.

8. C. Type the equal sign before you type the left parenthesis when you start to add a formula in the Formula Bar.

9. A. The CONCAT() function combines text strings in two or more cells and does not place a space or any other characters between each string.

10. D. You need to add a comma between each cell range in the parentheses within the SUM() function.

Chapter 5: Managing Charts

1. C. When you select the All Charts tab, a list of chart categories appears at the left side of the dialog box so that you can click each category and see the different types of charts that you can add to the right of the list.

2. B. Excel uses columns for the horizontal axis when there are an equal number of columns and rows.

3. A, C. You can change styles for both shapes and WordArt.

4. A. The legend appears at the bottom of the chart area so that you know what each color in the chart represents.

5. A, C, D. The built-in styles contain options for changing the border color, text color, and/or text background color.

6. C. When you click the Chart Elements icon in the upper-right corner of the selected chart, the right arrow appears when you move the mouse pointer over the element.

7. B. A chart in a chart sheet is a fixed size, even though sizing handles appear in the bounding box around the chart.

8. C. A trendline shows you the overall trend of one specific type of data over time.

9. D. A chart layout allows you to make changes to how the data is presented, and the chart style allows you to change the look and feel of the chart.

10. B. If you're sharing an Excel workbook online with other people in your company who may not be able to see the chart in your document, then Alt text is a great way to tell those people about the messages in your chart.

Index

Online Test Bank

Register to gain one year of FREE access after activation to the online interactive test bank to help you study for your Microsoft Office Specialist certification exam for Excel—included with your purchase of this book! All of the chapter review questions and the practice tests in this book are included in the online test bank so you can practice in a timed and graded setting.

Register and Access the Online Test Bank

To register your book and get access to the online test bank, follow these steps:

1. Go to bit.ly/SybexTest (this address is case sensitive)!
2. Select your book from the list.
3. Complete the required registration information, including answering the security verification to prove book ownership. You will be emailed a pin code.
4. Follow the directions in the email or go to www.wiley.com/go/sybextestprep.
5. Find your book on that page and click the "Register or Login" link with it. Then enter the pin code you received and click the "Activate PIN" button.
6. On the Create an Account or Login page, enter your username and password, and click Login or, if you don't have an account already, create a new account.
7. At this point, you should be in the test bank site with your new test bank listed at the top of the page. If you do not see it there, please refresh the page or log out and log back in.